Stitch by Stitch

Volume 16

TORSTAR BOOKS
NEW YORK · TORONTO

Stitch by Stitch

TORSTAR BOOKS INC.
300 E.42ND STREET
NEW YORK, NY 10017

Knitting and crochet abbreviations

approx = approximately	in = inch(es)	sl st = slip stitch
beg = begin(ning)	inc = increase(e)(ing)	sp = space(s)
ch = chain(s)	K = knit	st(s) = stitch(es)
cm = centimeter(s)	oz = ounce(s)	tbl = through back of
cont = continue(ing)	P = purl	loop(s)
dc = double crochet	patt = pattern	tog = together
dec = decreas(e)(ing)	psso = pass slipped	tr = triple crochet
dtr = double triple	stitch over	WS = wrong side
foll = follow(ing)	rem = remain(ing)	wyib = with yarn in
g = gram(s)	rep = repeat	back
grp = group(s)	RS = right side	wyif = with yarn in front
dc = half double	sc = single crochet	yd = yard(s)
crochet	sl = slip	yo = yarn over

A guide to the pattern sizes

		10	12	14	16	18	20
Bust	in	32½	34	36	38	40	42
	cm	83	87	92	97	102	107
Waist	in	25	26½	28	30	32	34
	cm	64	67	71	76	81	87
Hips	in	34½	36	38	40	42	44
	cm	88	92	97	102	107	112

Torstar Books also offers a range of acrylic book stands, designed to keep instructional books such as *Stitch by Stitch* open, flat and upright while leaving the hands free for practical work.

For information write to Torstar Books Inc., 300 E.42nd Street, New York, NY 10017.

Library of Congress Cataloging in Publication Data
Main entry under title:

Stitch by stitch.

Includes index.
1. Needlework. I. Torstar Books (Firm)
TT705.S74 1984   746.4   84-111
ISBN 0-920269-00-1 (set)

98765432

© Marshall Cavendish Limited 1984

Printed in Belgium

ISBN 0−920269−16−8   (Volume 16)

Step-by-Step Crochet Course

70 Decorative crochet edgings for the
        home 4
    Bobble edging
    Looped edging
    Stitch Wise: four edging patterns
    Patterns for edgings for a tablecloth
        and a window shade 9

71 Making crochet triangles 12
    Shaping with triangles
    Stitch Wise: square and triangle
        patterns
    Pattern for a casual coat 17

72 Circular ribbed motif 18
    Stitch Wise: two textured motifs
    Pattern for a woman's poncho ... 22

73 More about patchwork crochet 23
    Complete patchwork fabrics
    Patchwork made in strips
    Stitch Wise: patchwork patterns
    Pattern for a multi-colored sleeveless
        sweater 27

Step-by-Step Knitting Course

71 Knitting in rounds to make socks . 30
    Working ribbed socks with French
        heel and flat toe
    Patterns for children's socks 33

72 Mending knitting 34
    Reinforcing worn knitting
    Mending holes
    Stitch Wise: embossed stitches
    Pattern for a woman's sweater 37

73 More ideas for remodeling knitting . 39
    Replacing ribbing
    Adding fabric trimmings to knitting
    Pattern for a girl's party dress and
        jumper with fabric insert 43

74 Working method for spool knitting . 46
    Joining in a new ball of yarn or a
        different color
    Joining cord to form strips and a ring
    Pattern for a circular shoulder bag in
        spool knitting 48

75   Using spool knitting as cording   50
     Shape and color effects in spool
       knitting
     Pattern for a woman's sweater
       trimmed with cording   53

Step-by-Step Sewing Course

68   Conspicuous bound seams   55
     Easy binding
     Pattern for an evening jacket and bag:
       adapting the pattern   56
       directions for making   58

69   Making a seam roll   61
     Herringbone stitched hem
     Working with wool fabric
     Pattern for culottes: adapting the
       pattern   63
       directions for making   65

70   Pocket with welt   66
     Decorative snaps
     Pattern for a double-breasted blouse:
       adapting the pattern   68
       directions for making   70

71   Making an arrowhead tack   72
     Topstitched knife pleats
     Understitched knife pleats
     Pattern for a pleated dress: adapting
       the pattern   74
       directions for making   77

72   Working with knit fabrics   79
     Applying a cowl-neck collar with
       facings
     Pattern for a two-piece suit:
       adapting the pattern   80
       directions for making   83

Step-by-Step Needlework Course

19   Blackwork   85
     Some blackwork stitch patterns
     Designing blackwork
     A blackwork photograph album cover
       to make   87

Extra Special Crochet

     Woman's patterned jacket   89
     Lacy circular shawl   91
     Little girl's bathrobe   93

Extra Special Knitting

     Man's Fair Isle jacket   96
     Sleeveless top and jacket   100

Extra Special Sewing

     Draped dress or jumpsuit   103
     Girls' pinafores   108

Homemaker

     Pictures to knit and stitch   112
     Studio bedspread   116
     Suffolk puff crib quilt   119
     Baby sling   122
     Window valances   126

Shoestring

     Stuffed toy piglet   11
     Embroidered handkerchief   29
     Bathtub pillow   45

Crochet / COURSE 70

*Decorative crochet edgings for the home
*Bobble edging
*Looped edging
*Stitch Wise: four edging patterns
*Patterns for edgings for a tablecloth and a window shade

Decorative crochet edgings for the home

There are many crochet edgings which are ideal for trimming household items, including lampshades, window shades, tablecloths, bedspreads, pillows and chair covers. They can be sewn or glued to woven fabrics, as well as knitted or crocheted items.

A variety of yarns and materials can be used. You need not confine yourself to working with knitting yarns but should experiment with tubular rayon, glitter yarn, string and narrow ribbon, all available from most craft shops. Do, however, make sure that the yarn you choose is suitable

for the fabric to be trimmed; a lampshade should be trimmed with a light- or medium-weight cotton or rayon yarn so that the resulting edging is firm and light, while a heavy bedspread would need to be trimmed in a thicker yarn to prevent the edging from getting lost.

Bobble edging

The bobbles for this attractive edging are worked separately and attached to the heading once they have been completed. The size of the bobble can be varied by altering the number of stitches worked in the first round, then increasing and decreasing the bobble shape accordingly. Because the heading is worked as a separate piece you can use a variety of patterns to suit the article being trimmed: a simple single crochet or filet strip for a lampshade, for example, or a thick cluster pattern for a bedspread.

Use a smaller hook than normal when working both the heading and the bobbles (for knitting worsted use a size E [3.50mm] hook) in order to ensure a neat, firm finish.

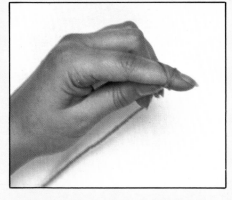

1 To make the bobbles, first wind the yarn around the first finger of the left hand once, keeping the cut end of yarn in the left hand.

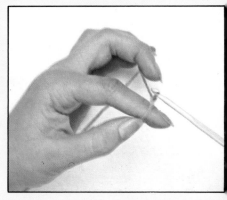

2 Now insert the hook under the yarn on finger, wind yarn over hook and draw through a loop.

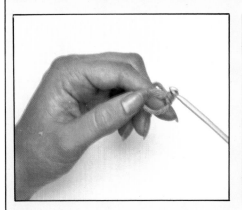

3 Slip circle off finger and hold it in left hand. Insert hook into circle, wind yarn over hook, draw through a loop, yarn over hook and through 2 loops on hook to complete first single crochet.

4 Work 7 more single crochets into circle. Now pull cut end of yarn tightly, thus pulling the stitches into a closed circle. This method can also be used whenever a small, invisible ring is required at the start of any circular crochet motif.

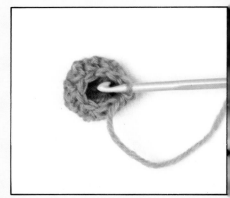

5 Continue making bobble by working 2 single crochets into each stitch on next round, then work one round without shaping. Shape on next round by working 2 stitches together all around. 8 single crochets.

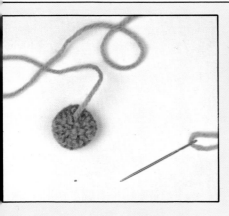

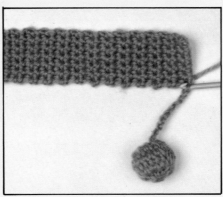

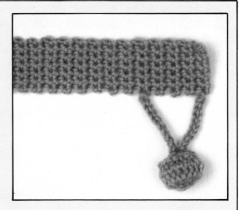

6 Stuff bobble firmly with absorbent cotton or another suitable padding, making sure that the bobble is a firm, round shape. Without breaking yarn, thread loop through remaining stitches and gather to close top.

7 The completed bobble can now be attached to any crochet edging. Here 6 single crochets have been worked in each row for a plain border. Work 9 chains. Join last chain to one side of border with a slip stitch at edge as shown here.

8 Slip stitch down these chains and into stitch at top of bobble. Repeat steps 7 and 8 once more, leaving at least 3 row ends between slip stitches on border. Fasten off yarn.

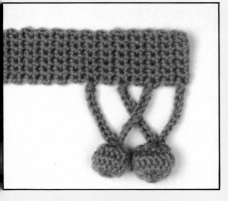

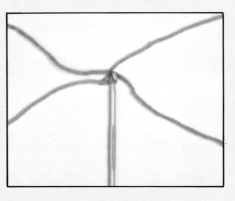

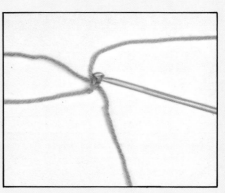

9 To complete edging, make another bobble and 9 chains. Slip stitch into border as before between chains just attached. Slip stitch down last 9 chains to bobble, make a further 9 chains and slip stitch into border, leaving same number of rows between slip stitches as before.

10 Complete bobble as before. Now continue to work bobbles and chains in this way, crossing over chains as shown here.

11 Here raised bobbles (see Volume 5, page 28) and single crochet have been combined for a textured edging, finished with a bobble fringe.

Looped edging

A looped edging is ideal for trimming chair covers, lampshades and bedspreads and is made by looping one yarn over another. You can use the same yarns for the loops and heading, or two different yarns for an unusual effect.

The yarns have been coded "A" and "B" for clarity, A being used for the loops and B for the heading.

You may find this edging difficult to work at first, but once mastered it is quite easy and very versatile; you can use many different yarns including tubular rayon and ribbon. Small beads threaded on the looped yarn before you start to work the edging make a very attractive border.

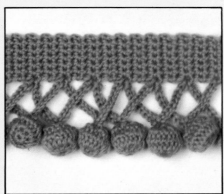

1 Use a smaller hook than usual for the best results. Using B make 1 chain. Hold A between hook and working loop with cut end in the left hand as shown here.

2 Now make one chain with B so that it holds A in place at back of work.

Mike Berend

continued

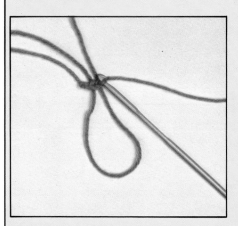

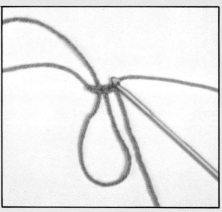

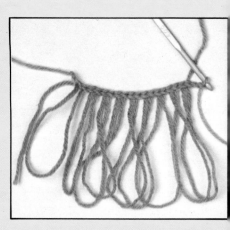

3 Loop A over B from right to left, leaving a long loop approximately 1½in (4cm) in length (when doubled). Work a chain in B to hold A in place.

4 Now take working loop end of A from right to left over B. Do not leave a loop this time. Work one chain in B to hold A in place as before.

5 Continue to make loops in this way with A for the length required, repeating steps 3 and 4 each time until edging is desired length. Break off A.

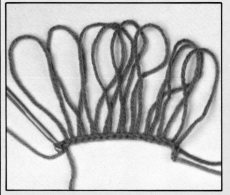

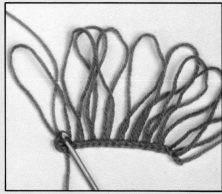

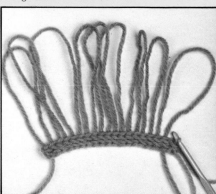

6 To widen the heading make 2 chains at end of loop row with B. Now turn edging so loops are at top, with right side facing and 3 chains just worked at left. Hold yarn at back of work.

7 Start working from left to right. Place hook between first two strands of first loop and work a slip stitch over first strand.

8 Continue to work a slip stitch over each strand of each loop, always working from left to right. Slip stitch into one chain at end of chain. Push the slip stitches up adjacent to first row if necessary and do not skip any loops.

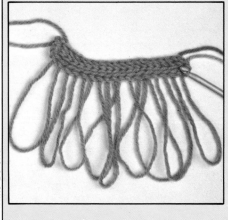

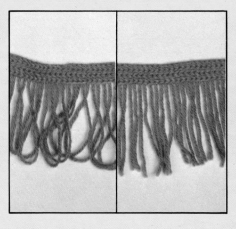

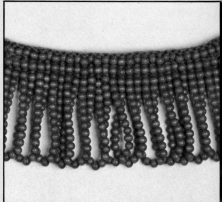

9 Make 3 chains. Turn work so that right side is facing and loops are at bottom once more. Hold 3 chains in left hand and work a slip stitch over each strand of each loop as before from left to right, pushing the slip stitches up to lie against previous row. Slip stitch into loop at edge of row. Repeat as required.

10 The loops can be either left uncut as shown at left or cut to form a fringe as shown at right. Make sure that the yarn used will not unravel if cut, *before* making the fringe.

11 Here beads have been threaded onto the loop yarn and the edging worked in the same way as before. Leave approximately 1in (2.5cm) of yarn between beads and hook and tighten looped yarn to ensure beads are evenly distributed.

Mike Berend

Stitch Wise

Diamond edging

Make 9ch.
1st row 1sc into 3rd ch from hook, 1sc into each ch to end. Turn.
2nd – 5th rows 1ch, skip first sc, 1sc into each sc to end working into back loop only of each st. Turn.
6th row Work as 2nd row to end of row. 8ch. Turn. Diamond completed.
Rep first 6th rows for length required, making 9 ch at end of last row. Do not turn.
Side edge
1st row 1sc into first free point of last diamond worked, *7ch, 1sc into free point of next diamond, rep from * to end, ending last rep with 5ch, 1tr into first ch of foundation ch. Turn.
2nd row (RS) 1ch, 1sc into first tr, 5sc into next 5-ch loop, *1sc into next sc, 7sc into next 7-ch loop, rep from * to end, ending with 1sc into next sc, 6sc into next 6-ch loop, turn.
3rd row 3ch, skip first sc, 1dc into next sc, 3ch, skip 3sc, *1dc into each of next 3sc, 5ch, skip 5sc, rep from * to end, ending with 1dc into each of next 3sc, 3ch, skip 3sc, 1dc into next sc, 1dc into turning ch. Turn.
4th row 1ch, skip first dc, 1sc into next dc, *work 3sc into each 5-ch loop and 1sc into each dc to end of row, working last sc into top of turning ch. Fasten off.

Spiral edging

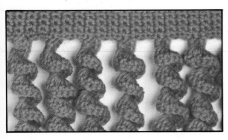

Make any length of chains.
1st row 1hdc into 3rd ch from hook, 1hdc into each ch to end. Turn.
2nd row (loop row) 1ch to count as first sc, skip first st, *work 1sc into next st, extend loop on hook for 4in (10cm), hold st being worked with left hand and twist yarn on hook approximately 24 times in clockwise direction, fold twisted yarn in half and work 1sl st into top of st just worked (hold twisted yarn at center if possible while working sl st), rep from * to end of row, working last sc into top of turning ch. Fasten off.

Fringed edging

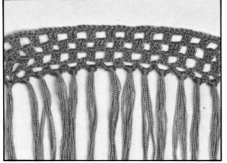

Make a multiple of 2 plus 1 chains with 1 extra turning chain.
1st row 1hdc into 3rd ch from hook, 1hdc into each ch to end. Turn.
2nd row 3ch to count as first hdc and 1ch sp, skip first 2hdc, 1hdc into next hdc, *1ch, skip next hdc, 1hdc into next hdc, rep from * to end, working last hdc into turning ch. Turn.
3rd row 2ch, skip first 1-ch sp, *1dc into next hdc, 1dc into 1-ch sp just skipped, keeping hook at front of work, skip next sp, rep from * to end, working last crossed group by working first dc of last group into top of turning ch, then 2nd dc of last group into sp just skipped. Turn.
4th row 3ch to count as first hdc and 1ch sp, skip first 2dc, 1hdc into next dc, *1ch, skip next dc, 1hdc into next dc, rep from * to end, working last hdc into top of turning ch. Fasten off. Take 6 strands of yarn approximately 8in (20cm) long (or as required), fold in half and knot into each 1-ch sp at lower edge if desired.

Twisted chain edging

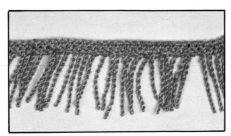

Make 6 chains.
1st row 1sc into 3rd ch from hook, 1sc into each ch to end. Turn. 4 sts.
2nd row 1ch to count as first sc, skip first st, 1sc into each st to end, 1sc into turning ch. Turn.
3rd row As 2nd.
4th row As 2nd. Do not turn. Work 24 chains. Turn.
5th row 3dc into 4th ch from hook, *4dc into next ch, rep from * to end of ch, 1sc into each sc to end, 1sc into top of turning ch. Turn.
2nd to 5th rows form patt and are rep throughout.

Double cluster fringed edging

Make a multiple of 4 plus 2 chains with 1 extra turning chain.
1st row 1sc into 3rd ch from hook, 1sc into each ch to end. Turn.
2nd row 3ch to count as first dc, skip first sc, 1dc into next sc, *2ch, skip 2sc, 1dc into each of next 2sc, rep from * to end, working last dc into turning ch. Turn.
3rd row 3ch to count as first dc, keeping last loop of each dc on hook work 3dc into first 2-ch sp, yo and draw through all loops on hook—called 1Cl—, *skip 2dc, 1Cl into next 2-ch sp, rep from * to end, 1dc into top of turning ch. Turn.
4th row 3ch to count as first dc, 1dc into sp between last dc and 1Cl in previous row, *2ch, 2dc into next sp between Cl, rep from * to last Cl, 1dc between last Cl and turning ch, 1dc into top of turning ch. Turn.
5th row 4ch, 1sc into first 2-ch sp, *4ch, 1sc into next 2-ch sp, rep from * to end working last sc into top of turning ch. Turn.
6th row 1ch to count as first sc, 2sc into first 4-ch loop, *1sl st into next sc, 3sc into next 4-ch loop, rep from * to end, 1sl st into turning ch. Fasten off. Knot a fringe into each 4-ch loop at lower edge if desired.

Ribbon threaded edging

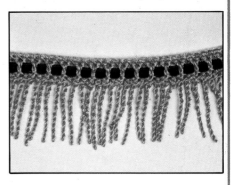

Work as for twisted chain edging, but working 1 row of doubles before loop row. Thread ribbon through doubles as shown here.

Tablecloth and window shade edgings

Add a touch of elegance to your home with these crochet edgings.

Tablecloth edging

Size
To fit a round tablecloth 80in (2m) in diameter.
Depth, 4¾in (12cm).

Note: To make edging for a larger or smaller tablecloth you can alter the length of the edging by working either more or fewer rows.

Materials
16oz (400g) or 1400yd (1280m) of a medium-weight mercerized crochet cotton
Size C (3mm) crochet hook
Round tablecloth 80in (2m) in diameter

Gauge
13 rows to 4in (10cm) worked in patt on size C (3mm) hook

To make
Using size C (3mm) hook make 30ch
Base row 1dc into 8th ch from hook, (2ch, skip 2 ch, 1dc into next ch) 3 times, 5ch, skip 12 ch, (1dc, 3ch) 3 times into last ch, 1dc into same ch. Turn.
1st row (RS) 1ch, (1sc, 1hdc, 1dc, 1tr, 1dc, 1hdc, 1sc) into each of three 3-ch sps—called make shamrock—5ch, 1dc into 5-ch sp, (2ch, 1dc into next dc) 4 times, 2ch, skip 2 ch, 1dc into next ch. Turn.
2nd row 5ch, skip first dc, 1dc into next dc, (2ch, 1dc into next dc) 4 times, 2ch, 1dc into 5-ch sp, 7ch, (1dc, 3ch) 3 times into tr in center of 2nd petal, 1dc into same place. Turn.
3rd row 1ch, make shamrock, 5ch, 1dc into 7-ch sp, (2ch, 1dc into next dc) 6 times, 2ch, skip 2 ch, 1dc into next ch. Turn.
4th row 5ch, skip first dc, 1dc into next dc, (2ch, 1dc into next dc) 6 times, 2ch, 1dc into 5-ch sp, 7ch, (1dc, 3ch) 3 times into tr in center of 2nd petal, 1dc into same place. Turn.
5th row 1ch, make shamrock, 5ch, 1dc into 7-ch sp, (2ch, 1dc into next dc) 8 times, 2ch, skip 2 ch, 1dc into next ch. Turn.
6th row 5ch, skip first dc, 1dc into next dc, (2ch, 1dc into next dc) 3 times, 5ch,

skip 4 sps, (1dc, 3ch) 3 times into next sp, 1dc into same sp. Turn.
The first to 6th rows form the patt. Rep these six rows until the edging is the required length, ending with a 5th row. Fasten off.

To finish
Press with a warm iron and a damp cloth. Then overcast the edging in place around the tablecloth. Overcast the end of the edging to the beginning.

Edging for a window shade

Size
To fit a 48in (122cm)-wide window shade.
Depth, 4in (10cm).
Note: Allow 6ch for each 2in (5cm) to be added or deducted to width.

Materials
4oz (100g) or 300yd (280m) of a lightweight mercerized crochet cotton
Sizes D and E (3.25 and 3.50mm) crochet hooks
Absorbent cotton balls
Window shade 48in (122cm)-wide

Gauge
12 spaces to 4in (10cm) worked on size E (3.50mm) hook.

To make heading
Using size E (3.50mm) hook make 291 ch loosely.

Base row 1dc into 4th ch from hook, 1dc into each ch to end. Turn.
1st row 4ch (to count as first dc and 1ch), skip next dc, 1dc into next dc, *1ch, skip next dc, 1dc into next dc, rep from * to end, working last dc into 3rd of the 4ch. Turn. 144 spaces.
2nd row 4ch, 1dc into next dc, *1ch, 1dc into next dc, rep from * to end, working last dc into 3rd of the 4ch. Turn.
Rep last row until work measures 2¼in (6cm) from beg.
Fasten off.

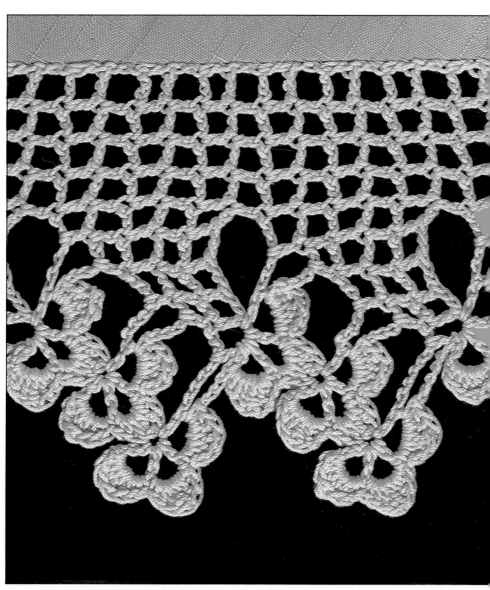

Bobble edging
First bobble

**Using size D (3.25mm) hook, wrap yarn once around first finger, insert hook into loop from underneath and work 8sc into loop, removing finger, tighten ring by pulling end of yarn.

Mark beg of each round with a colored thread.

Next round Work 2sc into each sc all around.

Next 2 rounds Work 1sc into each sc all around.

Stuff a small amount of cotton into bobble.

Next round (Work 2sc tog) 8 times.

Next round Work 1sc into each sc all around.**

Gather sts together by threading working st through each free st, do not cut off yarn but work *9ch, sl st into first dc on heading, sl st into each ch back to bobble, 9ch, skip next 5 dc, sl st into next dc, sl st back along ch to bobble. Fasten off and darn in end.

Second bobble

Work as first bobble from ** to **
Gather sts together by threading working st through each free st, do not cut off yarn but work *9ch, sl st into 4th dc on heading, sl st into each ch back to bobble, 9ch, sl st into 6th dc from first sl st of this bobble, sl st back along ch to bobble. Fasten off and darn in end.

Third bobble

Work as first bobble from ** to **
Gather sts together threading working st through each free st, do not cut off yarn but work *9ch, sl st into same dc as second arm of first bobble on heading (i.e. 7th dc), sl st into each ch back along ch to bobble, 9ch, sl st into 6th dc from first sl st of this bobble, sl st back along ch to bobble.

Fasten off and darn in end.

Rep in the same way all along the edging, overlapping the arms of the bobbles.

To finish

Press lightly. Slip stitch edging to bottom of shade.

Paul Williams

Shoestring

Our endearing piglet will appeal to the young at heart of every age.

Percy Pig

Finished size
About 8×5in (20×12cm). A seam allowance of ⅜in (1cm) has been included throughout.

Materials
- *Piece of printed fabric 14×11in (35×28cm)*
- *Piece of solid-color fabric 5×3in (12×8cm)*
- *Scrap of white felt*
- *Pipe cleaner*
- *Pair of ¾in-diameter goggle eyes*
- *¾in (3cm)-diameter curtain ring*
- *Black stranded embroidery floss*
- *Thick white yarn*
- *Suitable stuffing*
- *Matching thread*
- *Paper for patterns*

1 For the body pattern draw a rectangle 7×6in (18×15cm) on a piece of paper. Round off all corners: first mark a point 3½in (9cm) along one long side from one corner.
Mark a point 2¾in (7cm) from the same corner down the short side. Draw a curve from point to point around the corner. Repeat on the remaining three corners. Cut out the resulting oval.
2 Trace the pattern for the snout. Place the oval pattern on a piece of paper and place the snout on one short side of it. Draw around the oval and the snout to make the complete body pattern Cut out the pattern.
3 For the ear pattern, take a piece of paper and draw a triangle with a 1½in (4cm)-long base. Mark the height 2¾in (7cm) up from the center of the base. Join this point to the two ends of the first line, curving the lines outward to form the ear shape.
4 From printed fabric cut two bodies, two ears and four 2½in (6.5cm)-diameter circles for feet.
5 From solid color fabric cut out two ears.
6 Place bodies together with right sides facing. Pin, baste and stitch around edges, leaving a small opening at the top of the back to insert tail. Trim seam and turn body right side out. Stuff it firmly. Turn in opening edges and pin them together.
7 For the tail cut three 8in (20cm) pieces of white yarn. Braid the strands of yarn together in an ordinary three-strand braid round the pipe cleaner. Wind matching sewing thread around each end to hold the braid and pipe cleaner together; fasten off thread securely. Cut off excess yarn.

8 Push one end of the tail inside the body at the opening. Slip stitch the opening edges together, catching in the tail. Curl the tail as shown in the photograph.
9 Place one printed ear and one solid-color ear together with right sides facing. Pin, baste and stitch around curved sides, leaving straight base edges open. Trim seam and turn ear right side out. Turn in base edges and slip stitch them together.
10 Run a line of gathering stitches along base edge of ear. Gather up ear slightly and sew it to one side of the pig.
11 Repeat steps 9 and 10 to make and sew other ear in place on opposite side of the body.
12 Position the eyes on the pig, just

in front of the ears. Sew eyes in place.
13 Run a line of gathering stitches around one foot. Place a small amount of stuffing on wrong side of foot, then pull up gathering thread to enclose it. Fasten off thread securely.
14 Repeat step 13 to make three more feet in the same way.
15 Sew feet to the base of the pig.
16 From white felt cut an oval 1in (2.5cm) long for the nose. Trim one end to flatten it slightly. Pin, baste and blanket-stitch the nose to the end of the snout.
17 Using six strands of black embroidery floss, work two round nostrils in satin stitch on the nose.
18 Sew the curtain ring to the nose.

Spike Powell

John Hutchinson

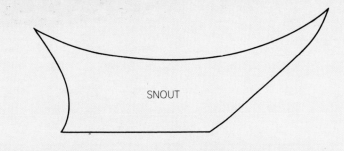

SNOUT

11

*Making crochet triangles
*Shaping with triangles
*Stitch Wise: square and
 triangle patterns
*Pattern for a casual coat

Making crochet triangles

A crochet triangle can be used not only by itself to create an unusual fabric, but also as a useful and effective aid when shaping a garment made from crochet squares. Thus crochet squares do not need to be confined to making bedspreads, shawls and blankets, but can be used for tops, jackets and cardigans.

Once you have mastered the basic technique for working the triangles, you should be able to work out triangle patterns for almost any square you wish to work, provided that the pattern is not too complicated to be cut in half at the center. You can use the same basic method whether you are working a very simple pattern or something more complicated, although you may find that where cluster groups, for example, are worked at the center of the square, you have to modify the pattern to achieve the correct triangular shape.

The triangle is started with a circle in the same way as when working a round motif. To achieve the correct shape you must work the remainder of the triangle in rows rather than rounds, working turning chains at the beginning of the row and turning the work at the end in the normal way. By working extra turning chains at the beginning of a row you can extend the base line of the triangle, thus creating the corners at each side to make the triangular shape. Where groups or clusters of stitches are worked at each side of the triangle, the extra chains will not be necessary.

As in many crochet patterns, a certain amount of trial and error is involved when working out the triangle pattern for any particular square, but it is worth the effort to achieve the exact shape.

The step-by-step pictures show you how to work a triangle to be used with a granny square (see Volume 3, page 9). The triangle is worked in rows rather than rounds to achieve the correct shape; the pattern must be worked in such a way that it matches the pattern on the square exactly. Use the same basic method for working any triangle to be used in conjunction with a particular square.

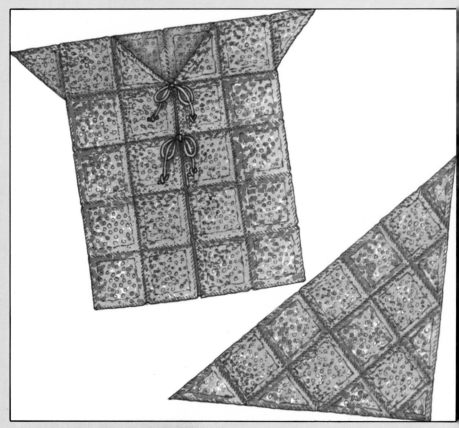

1 Baste a line across the center of the square with contrasting yarn from corner to corner. The base of the triangle will follow this line across the square and must be the same length. Use this method to start working out your own triangle instructions for any square.

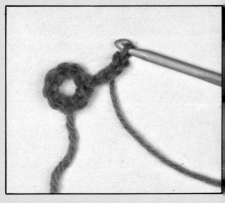

2 Start the triangle for the granny square with 8 chains joined into a circle with a slip stitch. Work in rows from now on. Make 4 chains. These count as the last double of the corner group at the side of the triangle and the first one-chain space between groups.

3 Now work 3 doubles, 2 chains and 3 doubles into the circle for the top point of the triangle. Complete the row with 1 chain and 1 double into the circle to act as the 1-chain space and first double of the last group at the side of the triangle.

4 Turn the triangle. Make 4 chains to count as the first corner as before. Now work 3 doubles into first chain space for first group on side of triangle.

5 Make 1 chain and then another corner group into 2-chain space at top of triangle. Complete row with 1 chain, 3 doubles into next 1-chain space, 1 chain, 1 double into 3rd of first 4 chains.

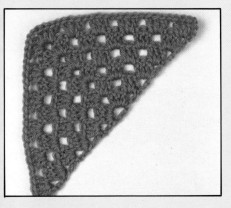

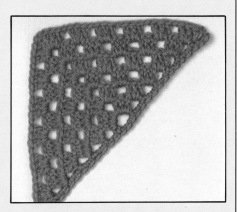

6 Turn. Continue to work each row in same way, with additional 3-double groups on each side of triangle, until you have worked same number of rows as rounds worked in square. Fasten off.

7 Place triangle over top half of square. You will see that it fits across center of square exactly with pattern matched on each row. Make sure that pattern matches in this way whichever square you choose.

8 A row of single crochets can be worked along the lower edge of the triangle if required to finish it, although this would not be necessary where a border is to be worked all around the edge of a garment. Make sure that the edge lies flat by working at least 2 single crochets into each row end.

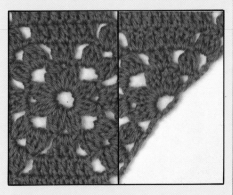

9 For a more complicated pattern, minor alterations may have to be made to the instructions to achieve the correct shape. In this square (on the left) a circle of clusters has been worked at the center. Working full clusters at the side corners will cause the triangle to dip as shown on the right.

10 To correct this, half cluster groups consisting of two doubles have been worked at the side corners of the triangles so that, once completed, the triangle base runs in a straight line and is the correct size for the square. (See page 17 for instructions on how to work the square.)

11 Similarly in this square 4 groups of 2 clusters have been worked at the center of the square (on the left), but only one complete group has been worked at the center of the triangle (on the right) with 2 half groups at each side to achieve the correct shape (see page 14.)

Mike Berend

13

Shaping with triangles

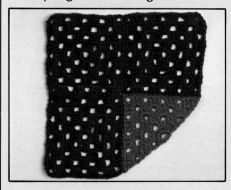 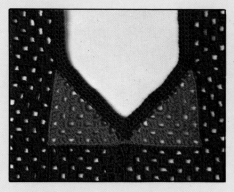 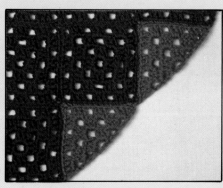

1 When using triangles in conjunction with squares it is a good idea to plan the pattern on paper first so that you can see where the triangles should be placed for the best effect. Crochet or sew triangles to squares as shown here.

2 By placing a triangle at each side of the neck you create a V-neck as shown. The same method can be used to shape the top of a cardigan or jacket. Work a border of single crochets or half doubles around the neck to finish the edges.

3 Use the triangles on the sides of a shawl where squares are placed in straight lines, by sewing the triangles up the sides of the shawl to give a straight side edge.

Stitch Wise

Cluster and double square

Make 8 ch. Join into a circle with sl st.
1st round 3ch to count as first dc, leaving last loop of each st on hook, work 2dc into circle, yo and draw through all loops on hook—called 2dcCl—, 5ch, leaving last loop of each st on hook, work 3dc into circle, yo and draw through all loops on hook—called 3dcCl—, *2ch, 3dcCl, 5ch, 3dcCl into circle, rep from * twice more, 2ch. Join with sl st to 3rd of first 3ch.
2nd round Sl st to first 5ch sp, 3ch, work (2dcCl, 2ch, 3dcCl) into same 5ch sp, *2ch, 3dc into next 2ch sp, 2ch, (3dcCl, 2ch, 3dcCl) into next 5ch sp, rep from * twice more, 2ch, 3dc into next 2ch sp, 2ch. Join with a sl st to 3rd of first 3ch.
3rd round Sl st into first 2ch sp, 3ch, work (2dcCl, 2ch, 3dcCl) into same sp, *2ch, 2dc into next 2ch sp, 1dc into each of next 3dc, 2dc into next 2ch sp, 2ch, (3dcCl, 2ch, 3dcCl) into next 2ch sp, rep from * twice more, 2ch, 2dc into next 2ch sp, 1dc

into each of next 3dc, 2dc into next 2ch sp, 2ch. Join with a sl st to 3rd of first 3ch.
4th round Sl st to first 2ch sp, 3ch, work (2dcCl, 2ch, 3dcCl) into same sp, *2ch, 2dc into next 2ch sp, 1dc into each dc worked in previous round, 2dc into next 2ch sp, 2ch, (3dcCl, 2ch, 3dcCl) into next 2ch sp, rep from * twice more, 2ch, 2dc into next 2ch sp, 1dc into each dc worked in previous round, 2dc into next 2ch sp, 2ch. Join with a sl st to 3rd of first 3ch. Fasten off. Rep 4th round to increase size of square, working 1dc into each dc worked in previous round and 2dc into 2ch spaces at each side.

Cluster and double triangle

Make 8ch. Join into a circle with sl st.
1st row 5ch to count as first dc and 2ch sp, leaving last loop of each st on hook, work 3dc into circle, yo and draw through all loops on hook—called 3dcCl—, 2ch, (3dcCl, 5ch, 3dcCl) into

circle (corner), 2ch, 3dcCl into circle, 2ch, 1dc into circle. Turn.
2nd row 5ch to count as first dc and 2ch sp, 3dcCl into first 2ch sp, *2ch, 3dc into next 2ch sp, 2ch, *(3dcCl, 2ch, 3dcCl) into next 5ch sp, rep from * to * once more, 3dcCl into last 2ch sp, 2ch, 1dc into 3rd of first 5ch. Turn.
3rd row 5ch to count as first dc and 2ch sp, 3dcCl into first 2ch sp, *2ch, 2dc into next 2ch sp, 1dc into each of next 3dc, 2dc into next 2ch sp, 2ch, *, (3dcCl, 2ch, 3dcCl) into next 2ch sp, rep from * to * once more, 3dcCl into last 2ch sp, 2ch, 1dc into 3rd of first 5ch.
4th row 5ch to count as first dc and 2ch sp, 3dcCl into first 2ch sp, *2ch, 2dc into next 2ch sp, 1dc into each dc worked in previous row, 2dc into next 2ch sp, 2ch, *, (3dcCl, 2ch, 3dcCl) into next 2ch sp, rep from * to * once more, 3dcCl into last 2ch sp, 2ch, 1dc into 3rd of first 5ch. Fasten off. To increase size of triangle repeat 4th row as for square.

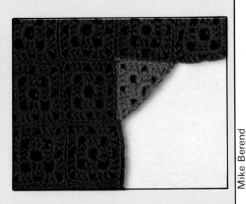

4 Where squares are placed so that they form a diamond pattern the triangles can be used to give a straight line at the top edge as shown here.

5 Use the triangles to form underarm shaping. Sew the triangle along one side of the last square in the sleeve and the last square at the top of the side seam on each side.

6 When the side and sleeve seams are joined together the triangles form a gently sloped shaping line at the underarm.

Mike Berend

Triple cluster square

Make 12ch. Join into a circle with sl st.
1st round 5ch to count as first tr and 1ch sp, work (1tr, 1ch) 15 times into circle. Join with a sl st to 4th of first 5ch. 16tr in circle.
2nd round Sl st to first 1ch sp, 3ch, leaving last loop of each st on hook work 3dc into same sp, yo and draw through all loops on hook—called 3dcCl—, *2ch, leaving last loop of each st on hook, work 4dc into next 1ch sp, yo and draw through all loops on hook—called 4dcCl—, rep from * into each 1ch sp to end of round, 2ch. Join with a sl st to 3rd of first 3ch.
3rd round Sl st to first 2ch sp, 3ch, 3dc into same sp, 2ch, 4dc into same sp (corner), *(3ch, 1sc into next 2ch sp) 3 times, 3ch, work (4dc, 2ch, 4dc) into next 2ch sp (corner), rep from * twice more, (3ch, 1sc into next 2ch sp) 3 times, 3ch. Join with a sl st to 3rd of first 3ch.
4th round Sl st into first 2ch sp, 3ch, into

same sp work (3dc, 2ch, 4dc), *1ch, skip first 3ch sp, (4dc into next 3ch sp, 1ch) twice, work (4dc, 2ch, 4dc) into next 2ch corner sp, rep from * twice more, 1ch, skip next 3ch sp, (4dc into next 3ch sp, 1ch) twice. Join with a sl st to 3rd of first 3ch.
5th round Sl st to first 2ch sp, 3ch, work (3dc, 2ch, 4dc) into same sp, *(4dc into next 1ch sp) 3 times, into next 2ch corner sp work (4dc, 2ch, 4dc), rep from * twice more, (4dc into next 1ch sp) 3 times. Join with a sl st to 3rd of first 3ch. Fasten off. To inc size of square rep 5th round, working 4dc into each 1ch sp on sides of square.

Triple cluster triangle

Make 12ch. Join into a circle with sl st
1st row 5ch to count as first tr and 1ch sp, *1tr, 1ch, rep from * 6 times more, 1tr into circle. Turn. 8 one-ch sps.
2nd row 5ch to count as first dc and 2ch

sp, *leaving last loop of each st on hook work 4dc into next 1ch sp, yo and draw through all loops on hook—called 4dcCl—, 2ch, rep from * into each sp all around, ending with 4dcCl into last 1ch sp, 2ch, 1dc into 3rd of first 5ch. Turn.
3rd row 5ch, 4dc into first 2ch sp, *(3ch, 1sc into next 1ch sp) 3 times, 3ch, *, (4dc, 2ch, 4dc) into next 2ch sp (corner), rep from * to * once more, 4dc into last 2ch sp, 2ch, 1dc into 3rd of first 5ch. Turn.
4th row 5ch, 4dc into first 2ch sp, *1ch, skip first 3ch sp, (4dc into next 3ch sp, 1ch) twice, *, 1ch, (4dc, 2ch, 4dc) into next 2ch sp, rep from * to * once more, 4dc into last 2ch sp, 2ch, 1dc into 3rd of first 5ch. Turn.
5th row 4ch, *4dc into first 2ch sp, *(4dc into next 1ch sp) 3 times, *, (4dc, 2ch, 4dc) into next 2ch sp (corner), rep from * to * once more, 4dc into last 2ch sp, 1ch, 1dc into 3rd of first 3ch. Fasten off. To increase size of triangle rep 5th round as for square.

Casual coat

This comfortable coat is easily made with lots of crochet squares and a few triangles for shaping.

Sizes

Coat To fit 34-36in (87-92cm) bust. Length, 35½in (89cm).
Sleeve seam, 10in (25cm).
Scarf Length 70in (175cm) excluding fringe.

Materials

57oz (1600g) of a bulky-weight yarn Sizes H and I (5.00 and 6.00mm) crochet hooks

Coat

Gauge

One square measures 5in (12.5cm) worked on size I (6.00mm) hook.

Square

Using size I (6.00mm) hook make 6ch, sl st into first ch to form a circle.
1st round 6ch to count as first dc and 3ch, 1dc into circle, *3ch, 1dc into circle, rep from * 5 times more, 3ch, sl st into 3rd of the 6.ch. 8 sps.
2nd round Sl st into first sp, 3ch to count as first dc, now leaving last loop of each on hook work 2dc into same sp as sl st, yo and draw through all loops on hook—called 2dc Cluster or 2dcCl—, *2ch, leaving last loop of each hook work 3dc into next sp, yo and draw through all loops

on hook—called 3dc Cluster or 3dcCl—, rep from * 6 times more, 2ch, sl st into top of 3ch.
3rd round Sl st into first sp, 2ch to count as first hdc, 2hdc, 3ch and 3hdc all into same sp as sl st—corner made—, *2ch, 2hdc into next sp, 2ch, 3hdc, 3ch and 3hdc all into next sp—corner made—, rep from * twice more, 2ch, 2hdc into next sp, 2ch, sl st into top of 2ch.
4th round Sl st to first corner sp, 2ch to count as first hdc, 2hdc, 2ch and 3hdc all into same corner sp, *(1ch, 3hdc into next sp) twice, 1ch, 3hdc, 2ch and 3hdc all into next corner sp, rep from * twice more, (1ch, 3hdc into next sp) twice, 1ch, sl st into top of 2ch. Fasten off.
Make 77 more squares.

Triangle

Using size I (6.00mm) hook make 6ch, sl st into first ch to form a circle.
1st row 6ch to count as first dc and 3ch, 1dc into circle, *3ch, 1dc into circle, rep from * twice more. Turn. 4 sps.
2nd row 3ch to count as first dc, 1dc into st at base of 3ch (half cluster), *2ch, 3dcCl into next sp, rep from * 3 times more, 2ch, 2dc into top of turning ch. Turn. 5 sps.
3rd row 2ch to count as first hdc, skip first dc, 1hdc into next dc, (2ch, 2hdc into next sp) twice, 2ch, 3hdc, 3ch and 3hdc all into next sp—corner made—, (2ch, 2hdc into next sp) twice, 2ch, 1hdc into next dc, 1hdc into top of turning ch. Turn.
4th row 3ch to count as first hdc and sp, *(3hdc into next sp, 1ch) 3 times, 3hdc, 2ch and 3hdc all into next sp—corner made—1ch, 1hdc into top of turning ch. Fasten off. Make 5 more triangles.

To finish

Darn loose ends on WS of motifs. Pin motifs to correct size and press or block, according to yarn used. Leave to cool before removing pins. Foll diagram for position of squares, overcast motifs tog, catching inner loop of corresponding sts on each square to form back, fronts and sleeves, then with WS facing join side and sleeve seams in same way leaving 10in (25cm) vent open at each side.

Border

With RS facing and using size H (5.00mm) hook, beg at center back neck and work 2 rounds sc around edges of coat including side vents, working 3 sc into each corner and sl st across top of side vents. Join each round with a sl st.
3rd round Work 1 sc into each sc all around, working 3 sc into corners and omitting side vents by breaking off yarn at lower edge and rejoining at other side of vent each time. Join with a sl st to first st. Fasten off.

Sleeve borders

Using size H (5.00mm) hook work 3 rounds of sc into edge of sleeves joining rounds with a sl st. Fasten off.
Press seams and borders lightly.

Ties

Using size I (6.00mm) hook and yarn double work a length of ch 10in (25cm) long. Fasten off. Work 3 more ties in same way and sew to front edges as shown.

Scarf

To make

Make 14 complete squares as for coat.

To finish

Press. Join squares into one long strip. Rejoin yarn to one corner sp and work sc around scarf, working 3 sc into each corner sp. Cut 30 pieces of yarn, each 12in (30cm) long, and knot 3 strands into each sp at each end of scarf.

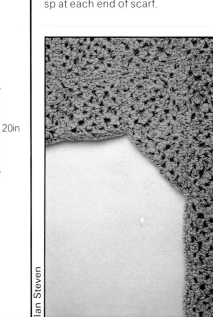

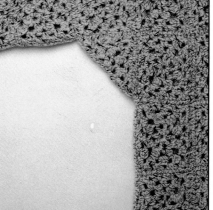

Ian Steven

Simon Butcher

Crochet / COURSE 72

*Circular ribbed motif
*Stitch Wise: two textured motifs
*Pattern for a woman's poncho

Circular ribbed motif

Our pictures in this course will help you to make the unusual ribbed motif used for the colorful poncho on page 21. For detailed instructions refer to the poncho pattern, using the pictures as a guide.

The center of the motif is worked in rounds in the usual way. The ribbed section is then worked in rows on this crochet motif, using "short row" shaping (see Volume 2, page 20) at the outer edge, thus fanning the ribs outward to achieve the circular shape.

To complete the motif you can then work two or more rounds onto the outer edge, working into the row ends of the ribbing and making the corners where indicated in the pattern.

The motif is most attractive when worked in knitting worsted or heavier yarn, and exciting effects can be achieved by using several different colors, working the ribbing in a narrow or wider striped pattern and using a contrasting color for the center motif and final rounds so that the ribs stand out in relief against the plain background.

1 The center of the motif is worked as a plain circle. Here 12 doubles have been worked in the first round, then 24 single crochets in the second round, by working two single crochets into each stitch worked in the previous round, for a medium-sized motif.

2 The ribbing is most effective when worked in at least one contrasting color. Cut off the first color at the end of the last round on the center motif and join on a second color. Make 9 chains (or the desired number) for the first ribbing row.

3 Work in rows from now on. 1 single crochet into 3rd chain from hook and every chain to center, then a slip stitch into same stitch where ribbing began on center motif, then turn work.

4 Work into the back loop only from now on. In order that ribbing will remain flat at the center, do not make a turning chain at the beginning of rows worked from the center outward. Skip the slip stitch and work a single crochet into each single crochet to the end of the row (including turning chain).

5 Now begin the "short row" shaping. Work 6 single crochets (including turning chain) in the usual way. Turn and work back to outer edge **without making a turning chain**, in order to maintain correct number of stitches.

6 Now turn and work 5 single crochets (including turning chain) along row. Complete shaping rows by working 6th single crochet into same stitch where row was turned.

7 Work a single crochet into each of the next two stitches. Now slip stitch into the **next** single crochet on the center motif, making sure that you work under two loops.

8 Repeat step 4 once more to the outer edge, then work a complete single crochet row back to center, working slip stitch into **next** single crochet on the center motif so that the ribbing is moved around the circle.

9 To continue working around the motif skip slip stitch at beginning of row and work one single crochet into each stitch to end, then repeat steps 5 to 8 once more.

10 Repeat step 9 all the way around the center motif, completing the ribbing by working a slip stitch into the last single crochet at the center and working back to the outer edge.

11 To join the two edges of the ribbed section together, leave a length of yarn sufficient to overcast the two sides together when it is fastened off. Overcast the two sides together on the wrong side, catching only one loop on each stitch to make an invisible seam.

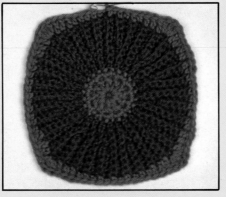

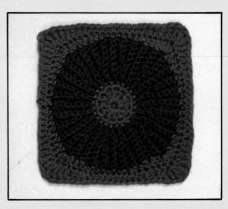

12 When using more than one color, you can obtain a neat joining by changing the yarn at the outer edge rather than the inner edge each time. If you intend to use the yarn again, do not carry it along the side edge of the work, as this would be too bulky, but reintroduce it once more when it is needed.

13 The final square shape is achieved by working two or more rounds (depending on size of motif required) around the outer edge. Rejoin the yarn to the right side of the ribbing and work into each row end. Because of the shape of the motif, this round will be graded, using single crochet, half doubles and doubles to achieve the correct shape.

14 Similarly the second round of the square will need to be graded, using half doubles, doubles and triples to ensure a good, square shape. For a larger motif the second round could be repeated several times, with more stitches worked on each side of the square each time.

Stitch Wise

Cluster and star motif

This motif measures approximately 8in (20cm) across when worked in sport yarn on a size E (3.50mm) hook.
Make 8ch. Join into a circle with a sl st.
1st round 7ch to count as first tr and 3ch sp, *1tr into circle, 3ch, rep from * 10 times more. Join with a sl st to 4th of first 7ch.
2nd round 4ch to count as first sl st and 3ch sp, *sl st into next tr, 3ch, rep from * 11 times more. Join with sl st to first ch.
3rd round Sl st into first 3ch sp, 3ch to count as first dc, work 3dc into same sp, drop working loop, insert hook from front to back through top of ch, draw working loop through to complete cluster—called 1 BCl—, 2ch, 4dc into same sp, drop working loop, insert hook into top of first dc from front to back, draw working loop through to complete cluster—4dcCl—, 2ch, *into next sp work (4dcCl, 2ch, 4dcCl), 2ch, rep from * 10 times more. Join with sl st to 3rd of first 3ch.
4th round Sl st into first 2ch sp, work (1 BCl, 5ch, 4dcCl) into same sp, (corner), 2ch, 3dc into next 2ch sp, 2dc into each of next 3 sps, 3dc into next sp, 2ch, *work (4dcCl, 5ch, 4dcCl) into next 2ch sp, (corner), 2ch, 3dc into next sp, 2dc into each of next 2 sps, 3dc into next sp, 2ch, rep from * twice more. Join with sl st to 3rd of first 3ch.
5th round Sl st into first 5ch sp, (1 BCl, 5ch, 4dcCl) into same sp, *3ch, work 3dc into next sp and complete cluster as before —called 3dcCl—, 2ch, leaving last loop of each st on hook work 1dc into each of next 2dc, yo and draw through all loops on hook (1dc dec)—called dec 1dc—, 1dc into each of next 8dc, dec 1dc, 2ch, 3dcCl into next 2ch sp, 3ch, (4dcCl, 5ch, 4dcCl) into next 5ch sp, rep from * twice more, 3ch, 3dcCl into next sp, 2ch, dec 1dc, 1dc into each of next 8dc, dec 1dc, 2ch, 3dcCl into last 2ch sp, 3ch. Join with a sl st to 3rd of first 3ch.
6th round Sl st into first 5ch sp, (1 BCl, 5ch, 4dcCl) into same sp, *(3ch, 3dcCl into next sp) twice, 2ch, dec 1dc, 1dc into each of next 6dc, dec 1dc, 2ch, (3dcCl

into next sp, 3ch) twice, (4dcCl, 5ch, 4dcCl) into next 5ch sp, rep from * twice more, (3ch, 3dcCl into next sp) twice, 2ch, dec 1dc, 1dc into each of next 6dc, dec 1dc, 2ch, (3dcCl into next sp, 3ch) twice. Join with a sl st to 3rd of first 3ch.
7th round Sl st into first 5ch sp, (1 BCl, 5ch, 4dcCl) into same sp, *(3ch, 3dcCl into next sp) 3 times, 2ch, dec 1dc, 1dc into each of next 4dc, dec 1dc, 2ch, (3dcCl into next sp, 3ch) 3 times, (4dcCl, 5ch, 4dcCl) into next 5ch sp, rep from * twice more, (3ch, 3dcCl into next sp) 3 times, 2ch, dec 1dc, 1dc into each of next 4dc, dec 1dc, 2ch, (3dcCl, 3ch, into next sp) 3 times. Join with a sl st to 3rd of first 3ch.
8th round Sl st into first 5ch sp, (1 BCl, 5ch, 4dcCl) into same sp, *(3ch, 3dcCl into next sp) 4 times, 2ch, dec 1dc, 1dc into each of next 2dc, dec 1dc, 2ch, (3dcCl into next sp, 3ch) 4 times, (4dcCl, 5ch, 4dcCl) into next 5ch sp, rep from * twice more, (3ch, 3dcCl into next sp) 4 times, 2ch, dec 1dc, 1dc into each of next 2dc, dec 1dc, 2ch, (3dcCl in next sp, 3ch) 4 times. Join with a sl st to 3rd of first 3ch.
9th round Sl st into first 5ch sp, (1 BCl, 5ch, 4dcCl) into same sp, *(3ch, 3dcCl into next sp) 5 times, 2ch, leaving last loop of each st on hook work 1dc into each of next 4dc, yo and draw through all loops on hook—called 4dc dec—, 2ch, (3dcCl into next sp, 3ch) 5 times, (4dcCl, 5ch, 4dcCl) into next 5ch sp, rep from * twice more, (3ch, 3dcCl into next sp) 5 times, 2ch, 4dc dec, 2ch, (3dcCl into next sp, 3ch) 5 times. Join with sl st to 3rd of first 3ch.
10th round Sl st to first 5ch sp, 1ch to count as first sc, (2sc, 2ch, 3sc) into same sp, *work 2sc into each sp, and 1sc into top of each cluster and 4dc into next 5ch sp, (3sc, 2ch, 3sc) into next 5ch sp, rep from * twice more, work 2sc into each sp and 1sc into top of each cluster and 4dc dec group to end. Join with sl st to first ch. Fasten off.

Twisted doubles motif

This motif measures approximately 7in (17cm) across when worked in knitting worsted on a size G (4.50mm) hook.
Make 6ch. Join into a circle with a sl st.
1st round 2ch, *(yo and insert hook into circle, yo and draw up a loop) 3 times, yo and draw through first 6 loops on hook, yo and draw through rem 2 loops on hook (small bobble), rep from * 5 times more. Join with a sl st to 2nd of first 2ch.
2nd round 5ch to count as first hdc and 3ch sp, *1hdc between next 2 bobbles, 3ch, rep from * 4 times more. Join with a sl st to 2nd of first 5ch.
3rd round 2ch, *(yo and insert hook into next 3ch sp, yo and draw up a loop) 5 times, yo draw through first 10 loops,

yo and draw through rem 2 loops on hook —large bobble—3ch, large bobble into same sp, 3ch, rep from * 11 times more. Join with a sl st to 2nd of first 2ch.
4th round *3ch, work 1sc between next 2 bobbles inserting hook under 3ch loop worked in 2nd round drawing 2nd and 3rd round loops tog, rep from * to end. Join with a sl st to first of first 3ch.
5th round Sl st into first 3ch sp, 3ch to count as first dc, (2dc, 3ch, 3dc) into same sp, 2dc into each of next two 3ch sps, *(3dc, 3ch, 3dc) into next sp (corner), 2dc into each of next two 3ch sps, rep from * twice more. Join with a sl st to 3rd of first 3ch.
6th round Sl st into first 3ch sp, (2ch, 2hdc, 2ch, 3hdc) into same sp, *(inserting hook behind stem of next st from right to left and to front again work 1dc—called 1dcF—, inserting hook from right to left around front of stem of next st and to back again work 1dc—called 1dcB—) 5 times, (3hdc, 3ch, 3hdc) into next sp, rep from * twice more, (1dcF, 1dcB) 5 times. Join with a sl st to 2nd of first 2ch.
7th round Sl st into first sp, 2ch, (2hdc, 3ch, 3hdc) into same sp, beg with 1dcB work *(1dcB, 1dcF) alternately around stem of each of next 3hdc, 13dc and 3hdc to next corner (3hdc, 3ch, 3hdc) into next sp, rep from * twice more, work 1dcB then 1dcF alternately around stem of each of next 3hdc, 13dc and 3hdc. Join with a sl st to 2nd of first 2ch.
8th round Work as given for 7th round but starting each side of square with 1dcF around first hdc worked in previous round, then working 1dcB then 1dcF alternately around stem of each hdc and dc worked in previous round, working corner groups as before.
9th round Sl st into first 3ch sp, 3ch, (2dc, 3ch, 3dc) into first sp, *skip first 2 sts, 1dc into next st, 1dc into each dc worked in previous round, 1dc into next st, skip 2sts, (3dc, 3ch, 3dc) into next sp, rep from * twice more, skip 2sts, 1dc into each dc worked in previous round, 1dc into next hdc, skip 2hdc. Join with a sl st to 3rd of first 3ch.
10th round As 9th. Fasten off.

Woman's poncho

We've used colors that echo the falling leaves of autumn in this poncho. It will keep out cold winds all winter.

Size
56¼in (145cm) square.

Materials
- 29oz (800g) of a knitting worsted in main color (A)
- 9oz (250g) in 1st contrasting color (B)
- 8oz (200g) in each of 2nd, 3rd, 4th, 5th and 6th contrasting colors (C, D, E, F and G)
- Size H (5.00mm) crochet hook

Gauge
One motif measures 7¾in (20cm) square worked on size H (5.00mm) hook.

Motif
Using size H (5.00mm) hook and A, make 6ch, sl st, into first ch to form a circle.
1st round 3ch to count as first dc, work 11dc into circle, sl st into top of 3ch. 12dc.
2nd round 1ch to count as first sc, 1sc into base of ch, 2sc into each st all around, sl st into first ch. 24sc.
Cut off A. Join on B. Beg patt, working in rows into back loop only of each st to form ribbing.
Base row 9ch. Turn.
1st row 1sc into 3rd ch from hook, 1sc into each ch to end, sl st into same place as last sl st on center motif. Turn.
2nd row Skip sl st, 1sc into each sc to end, 1sc into turning ch. Turn.

3rd row 1ch, 1sc into each of next 5sc, turn, skip first sc, 1sc into each of next 4sc, 1sc into turning ch, turn.
4th row 1ch, 1sc into each of next 4sc, 1sc into same st as last st worked on turning row—this completes shaping section—, 1sc into each of next 2sc, sl st into next sc on center motif. Turn.
5th row As 2nd.

6th row 1ch, 1sc into each sc to end, sl st into next sc on center motif. Turn.
7th row As 2nd.
8th row As 3rd.
9th row As 4th.
10th row As 2nd.
Cut off B, join on C and work rows 6 to 10 twice. Cont to work rows 6 to 10 working 10 rows in each of D, E, F and G, so finishing at outer edge. Fasten off leaving a long end. Taking one loop only into seam, join ends of motif. Rejoin A to outer edge of motif at start of B, 1ch, 1sc into each of next 2 row ends, *1hdc into each of next 3 row ends, 1dc into each of next 3 row ends, 3dc into next row end—corner formed—, 1dc into each of next 3 row ends, 1hdc into each of next 3 row ends, 1sc into each of next 5 row ends, rep from * to end, finishing 1sc into each of last 2 row ends, sl st into first ch.
Next round 2ch, 1hdc into each of next 4 sts, *1dc into each of next 4 sts, 1tr into first of the 3dc at corner, 3tr into next corner dc, 1tr into last corner dc, 1dc into each of next 4 sts, 1hdc into each of next 9 sts, rep from * to end, finishing 1hdc into each of last 4 sts, sl st into top of 2ch. Fasten off.
Make 47 more motifs, but join A to beg of next color—i.e. for the 2nd motif join A to beg of C section, for 3rd motif join A to beg of D section etc. Sew motifs tog in 7 rows of 7 motifs, leaving hole at center of middle row for neck.

Neck edging
Join on A and using size H (5.00mm) hook work 2 rows of hdc evenly all around neck.

Outer edging
Join on B and using size H (5.00mm) hook work 1 row of hdc evenly all around outer edge, working 3 hdc at each corner, then work 1 round in A. Fasten off.

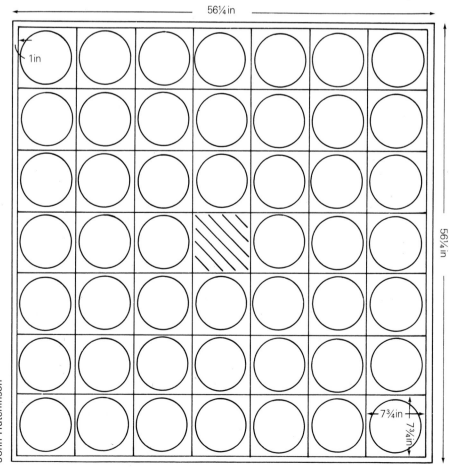

56¼ in

56¼ in

1in

7¾in

7¾in

Crochet / COURSE 73

*More about patchwork crochet
*Complete patchwork fabrics
*Patchwork made in strips
*Stitch Wise: patchwork patterns
*Pattern for a multi-colored sleeveless sweater

More about patchwork crochet

You have already learned how to make patchwork with different shaped pieces—squares, rectangles and hexagons for example—which can be sewn or crocheted together to form the fabric.

You can also make patchwork in two other ways: by making the fabric in one complete piece, using graph paper to plan the design and working the fabric in bright-colored blocks or stripes, or by making long strips, divided up into different colors, and sewing the strips together for the patchwork effect. Blocks, stripes and diamond shapes can all be worked in a variety of colors in the strips to create exciting and original patchwork designs.

The first method is ideal for making garments, since detailed shaping can be worked on the sides of the fabric for armhole, shoulder or sleeve shaping, and at the center for neck shaping. The strip method should only be used for something like a bedspread or rug, on which no shaping is required.

Use single crochet, half doubles or doubles for the best results.

Complete patchwork fabrics

A patchwork-style fabric that is made in one piece should be planned carefully before you start in order to make sure that the colors and shapes fit into the design of the garment. You need not merely repeat one shape in the design, but can combine large blocks, narrow strips, diamonds or hexagons in the fabric, provided that you plan carefully first and fit each section in carefully. To avoid making a really thick fabric, it is best to use separate balls of yarn for each color or block of color, twisting the yarn at the end of each section when it is being joined to avoid making a hole in the fabric (see Volume 2, page 20). Concentrate on using color to create interest, rather than complicated stitch patterns, which detract from the overall effect of the patchwork.

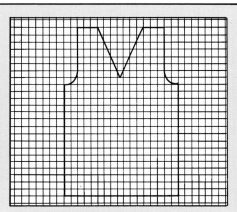

1 Make a gauge sample in the yarn of your choice, then start planning your patchwork garment by drawing the basic shape to scale on a piece of graph paper. Use paper with small squares, so that the complete shape can be seen.

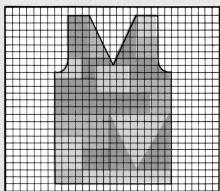

2 Color in the patchwork design, using the same colors that you intend to use for the design where possible. Take into account the stitch to be used. You will work more rows in single crochet than you will in half doubles or doubles, for example.

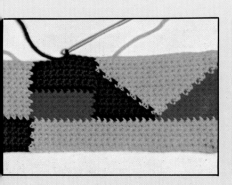

3 You can then work the pattern from the graph. If you are making a garment, complete the main fabric first, adding the ribbing or any borders at a later stage.

4 When planning the design try to make sure that fairly large blocks of color are placed at the side edges, so that when you are shaping the armhole, for example, you will not need to keep changing color while decreasing stitches.

5 Similarly, when planning a sleeve in a patchwork pattern, extend the color blocks at the side over the shaping, rather than adding new, narrow blocks, requiring a color change over just a few increased stitches.

Mike Berend

Patchwork made in strips

Working in strips is one of the simplest forms of patchwork crochet. Using this method, you can combine stripes, blocks of color and diagonal patterns in many different ways to create unusual patchwork patterns. Remember to plan the design carefully before you start, making sure that the colors complement each other and that the strips, when sewn together, create an ordered, rather than a haphazard-looking fabric.

Use the strips to make vividly colored and interestingly textured rugs, bedspreads and afghans, using different yarns as well as different colors for really unusual fabrics.

1 The simplest pattern uses variegated stripes divided into blocks with one dark color. By reversing the colors on the strips you create the patchwork effect. For bands of color with an even number of rows the yarn can be carried up the side of the work (as in the sample on the left); for uneven bands it must be broken off and rejoined (as in the sample on the right).

2 Use the dark color to overcast or crochet the strips together, so that each block of color is outlined in the darker shade, emphasizing the patchwork pattern.

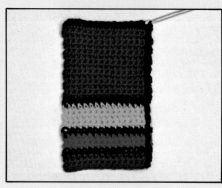

3 A slip stitch edging worked down the side of each strip is an unusual way of joining the pieces together. Make a loop on the hook and insert the hook into the bottom corner of the strip. Draw a loop through and through the loop on the hook.

4 Now insert the hook into the next hole up on the very edge of the work and draw a loop through this hole and the loop on the hook. Continue to work slip stitches up the side of the strip. Make sure you pull the yarn through **loosely** to avoid making a hard, tight edge.

5 Work slip stitch up left-hand side of second strip in same way; then overcast the strips together on the WS using same color yarn as for slip stitches, but do not catch the slip stitches while sewing the pieces together.

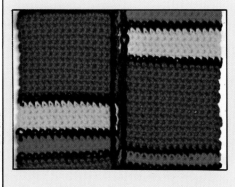

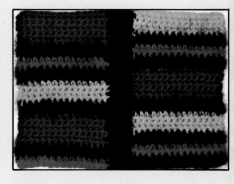

6 On the right side the slip stitches form two parallel lines on the strips.

7 For a more unusual effect use a mohair yarn for the unifying dark lines of the patchwork. Use the mohair within the strips as shown.

8 Make narrow strips in the mohair about one-fourth to one-third the width of each patterned strip and join the pieces together by sewing the narrow mohair strips down each side of the patterned strips.

Mike Berend

Stitch Wise

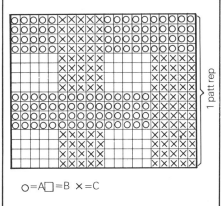

Woven strips

Make several strips, working from the chart, and sew them together for the woven effect.

O = A □ = B ✕ = C

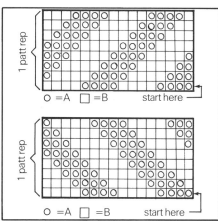

Diagonal strips

Alternate the two strips, changing colors to produce a staggered diagonal pattern.

O = A   □ = B   start here →

O = A   □ = B   start here →

1 patt rep

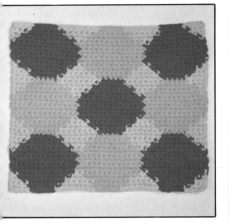

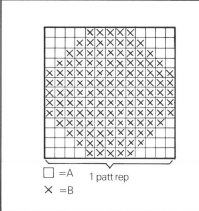

Octagons

Make a multiple of 13 ch, plus correct number of turning chains for stitch being used, and work patt from chart.

□ = A   1 patt rep
✕ = B

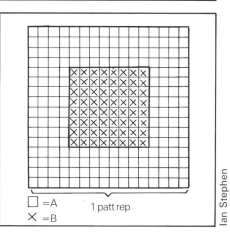

3-D squares

Make a multiple of 16ch plus correct number of turning chains for stitch being used, and work patt from chart.

□ = A   1 patt rep
✕ = B

Ian Stephen

Multi-colored sleeveless sweater

Give the classic sleeveless sweater a new lease on life by making it in patchwork crochet. Use a yarn that comes in a wide variety of colors, and you'll have a sweater to team with your entire wardrobe. It will be the most useful garment you own.

Sizes
To fit 34[36:38]in (87[92:97]cm) bust.
Length, 21½[22¼:23]in (54[56:58]cm).
Note Directions for larger sizes are in brackets [ ]; if there is only one set of figures it applies to all sizes.

Materials
9[11:11]oz (250[300:300]g) of a knitting worsted in main color
1oz (25g) in each of 6 contrasting colors – see chart
Sizes G and H (4.50 and 5.00mm) crochet hooks

Gauge
14 hdc and 12 rows to 4in (10cm) worked on size H (5.00mm) hook.

Front
Using size G (4.50mm) hook and main color make 65[69:73]ch.
Base row 1sc into 3rd ch from hook, 1sc into each ch to end. Turn. 64[68:72] sts. Work 5 more rows in sc.
Change to size H (5.00mm) hook. Work in hdc, starting each row with 2ch to count as first hdc, and working in patt from chart until the 37 rows of chart have

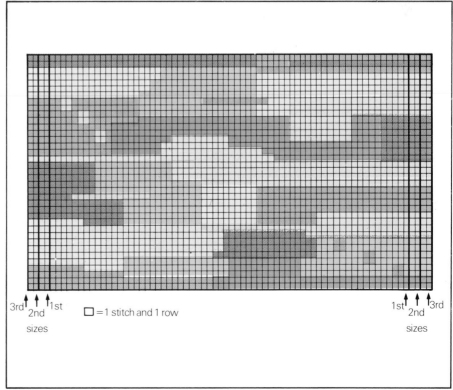

3rd 2nd 1st   □ =1 stitch and 1 row   1st 2nd 3rd
sizes   sizes

Ian Stephen

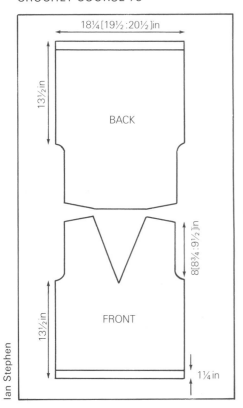

18¼[19½:20½]in

13½in

BACK

8[8¾:9½]in

13½in

FRONT

1¼in

Ian Stephen

been completed. Cut off yarns.**
Shape armholes and divide for neck
1st row With WS facing skip first 2 sts,
rejoin main color to next hdc, 2ch, 1hdc
into each of next 28[30:32] hdc, turn and
cont on these sts for first side of neck.
Cont in main color only, work 1 row, then
dec one hdc—by working 2hdc tog—at
each end of next row and foll 3 alternate
rows. Cont to dec at neck edge only on
every other row until 15[16:17] sts rem.
Cont straight until armhole measures
8[8¾:9½]in (20[22:24]cm); end at
armhole edge.
Shape shoulder
Next row Sl st over first 5[5:6] sts, patt
to end. Turn.
Next row Patt to within last 5[5:6] sts.
Fasten off.
Return to where work was left, with WS
facing skip center 2 sts, rejoin main
color to next st, 2ch, 1hdc into each
hdc to within last 2hdc, turn.
Cont to match first side reversing shaping.

Back
Work as for front to **.
Shape armholes
Next row With WS facing skip first 2 sts,
rejoin main color to next hdc, 2ch, 1hdc
into each hdc to within last 2hdc, turn.
Dec one hdc at each end of foll 4
alternate rows. 52[56:60] sts. Cont
straight until armholes measure same as
back to shoulders.
Shape neck and shoulders
Next row Sl st over first 5[5:6] sts, 2ch,
1hdc into each of next 9[10:10] hdc,
turn.
Next row Patt to within last 5[5:6] sts.

Fasten off.
Skip center 22[24:26] sts, rejoin yarn
to next st, 2ch, 1hdc into each hdc to
within last 5[5:6] sts, turn.
Next row Sl st over first 5[5:6] sts, 1hdc
into each hdc to end. Fasten off.

Neckband
Join shoulder seams. Using size G
(4.50mm) hook and main color and with
RS facing work a row of sc around neck
edge, working 1sc into each hdc along
back neck and 28[29:30]sc down each
side of front neck, sl st into first sc, turn.

Turning after each round, work 3 more
rounds in sc, dec one st at each side of
center front on each row. Fasten off.

Armhole borders (alike)
Using size G (4.50mm) hook and main
color work 58[62:66] sc evenly all
around armhole.
Turn and work 3 more rows in sc.
Fasten off.

To finish
Press or block, according to yarn used.
Join side seams.

Shoestring

Pocket hanky

Turn a plain handkerchief into something special with delicate embroidery in lilac and blue.

Finished size
About 9in (23cm) square.

Materials
- 12in (30cm) square of white lawn
- 8in (20cm) square of pale lawn
- One skein each of stranded embroidery floss in delphinium blue, cobalt blue and lilac
- Tracing paper
- Dressmaker's carbon paper
- Matching sewing thread
- 6in(15cm)-diameter embroidery hoop
- Medium-size crewel needle

1 Trace the butterfly wings from the corner design. Using dressmaker's carbon, trace the wings on the center of the blue fabric.
2 Mount the blue fabric in the hoop.
3 Using cobalt blue embroidery floss (three strands, as for the entire motif), work buttonhole stitch around each wing. Work two small eyelets on each wing. Using delphinium blue, complete the wings with backstitch veins and French knots.
4 Remove the fabric from the embroidery hoop and press it carefully on the wrong side.
5 With sharp-pointed scissors, carefully cut around the wings, keeping as close to the line of embroidery as possible.
6 Trace the complete motif, except for the wings. Transfer the motif onto one corner of the white lawn, far enough in from the corner so that the fabric will fit into the hoop.
7 Mount the fabric in the hoop. Pin and baste the wings in place. Using delphinium blue, work satin stitch across the body, catching in the wings.
8 Still using delphinium, work buttonhole stitch around the border of the motif. Work French knots in cobalt blue and lilac next to the edging. Using lilac, work leaves and butterfly head in satin stitch and work the eyelets. Using cobalt blue, backstitch along the remaining lines, and work French knots around the flowers.
9 Remove the completed embroidery from the hoop and press it carefully on the wrong side.
10 With sharp-pointed scissors, carefully cut around the scalloped edge.
11 Cut away the excess fabric from the remaining edges, leaving a 9½in (24cm) square.
12 Work a hand-rolled hem from the embroidered corner all around the remaining edges of the handkerchief.

Belinda

Ian Stephen

*Knitting in rounds to make socks
*Working ribbed socks with French heel and flat toe
*Patterns for children's socks

Knitting in rounds to make socks

Once you have mastered the art of knitting in rounds with four needles you can easily make socks. Socks can be in plain stockinette stitch, ribbed or patterned. They are usually knitted in sport yarn for ordinary wear. It is possible to buy special sock yarn, which is a mixture of wool for warmth and synthetic fibers for strength. When making children's socks, choose a machine-washable yarn.

There are four main sections in a sock— leg, heel, foot and toe.

The leg is worked in rounds and usually has a ribbed top, often a turned-down one. If the leg is in stockinette stitch, it needs shaping to narrow it toward the ankle. Ribbed socks do not require shaping as they have an elastic fabric.

At the ankle the stitches are divided in two. Leaving one half of the stitches for the instep, you work the heel in rows of stockinette stitch over the other stitches. Turning rows form the shaping on the heel so that it "turns" under the foot.

There are a number of different types of heel shaping. The French heel is very popular (see ribbed socks on page 33) as is the Dutch heel of the patterned socks.

After the heel is complete, the foot is worked in rounds, although it consists of two sections, the upper and lower foot. There is additional shaping on the lower part of the foot to reduce these stitches to the same number as those in the top. A flat toe is the most popular shape. The step-by-step pictures here are based on the instructions for the smallest size ribbed sock.

Working ribbed socks with French heel and flat toe

1 For comfort the turnover top is knitted in stockinette stitch with a narrow border of K1, P1 ribbing to produce a firm edge and to prevent the work from curling. This section includes a stripe sequence, which can be worked in school colors.

2 Before starting the main pattern, turn the work inside out to reverse the K1, P1 top so that it is on the correct side when turned over.

3 Continue in rounds of K2, P2 ribbing for required length to where work is divided for heel (about ankle level). No shaping is necessary for the leg as it is a ribbing pattern.

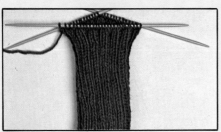

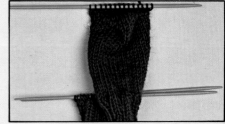

4 To work the heel, divide the total number of stitches by four. Here there are 52 stitches in the leg. Knit first 14 stitches in round, then slip last 12 stitches of round onto other end of this needle: these 26 stitches are for heel (facing you here). Divide remaining 26 stitches between 2 needles and leave for instep.

5 Beginning and ending with a purl row, work in rows of stockinette stitch on the heel stitches for 2¼in (6cm). There should be about the same number of rows of stockinette stitch as there are stitches on the needle.

6 Shape or "turn" the heel. **Next row** K14, sl 1, K1, psso, turn. **Next row** Sl 1, P2 tog, turn. **Next row** Sl 1, K3, sl 1, K1, psso, turn. **Next row** Sl 1, P4, P2 tog, turn. Continue to work one more stitch in this way on every row until all the stitches have been worked and 14 stitches remain, ending with a purl row.

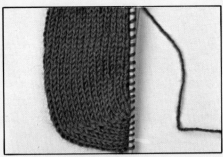

7 Knit back across half the stitches (here it is 7) to complete the heel. The heel shaping forms a triangle from the center of the heel outward: when the completed sock is folded flat the heel is rounded and the stitches have changed direction to fit under the foot.

8 Start picking up stitches to work the foot. First slip the instep stitches back onto one needle so that you have a spare needle. Use the spare needle to knit across the remaining 7 heel stitches, then pick up and knit 15 stitches up one side of the heel.

9 Using the next (second) needle, rib across the instep stitches. The main part of a sock (including the instep) may be plain, ribbed or patterned, but the heel under part of the foot and toe is always in stockinette stitch.

10 Continue picking up stitches for the foot. With the third needle, knit up 15 stitches down the other side of the heel, then knit across the 7 heel stitches. There are now 70 stitches on the 3 needles for the foot with the rounds beginning and ending in the middle of the under part of the foot.

11 Continue to work the foot in rounds. The first and third needles hold the instep stitches; you must decrease these on following alternate rounds — (first needle, K to last 3 sts, K2 tog, K1; 2nd needle, rib to end; 3rd needle, K1, sl 1, K1, psso, K to end) — to reduce these stitches to about the same number as the ribbed stitches for the top of the foot on the 2nd needle.

12 When 50 stitches remain, continue without shaping until the foot is the required length from the back of the heel: here it is 4¾in (12cm). Begin the toe shaping. Work in stockinette stitch and on the next and alternate rounds shape as follows: first needle, K to last 2 sts, K2 tog; 2nd needle, K1, sl 1, K1, psso, K to last 3 sts, K2 tog, K1; 3rd needle, sl 1, K1, psso, K to end.

13 The toe shaping is in two sections—a top and lower part with shaping at each side decreasing toward a straight section across the top of the toes. The 2nd needle holds the stitches for the top part of the toe while the first and 3rd needles hold the stitches for the lower part.

14 The toe shaping is complete when 18 stitches remain. Knit the stitches from the first needle onto the 3rd: now the stitches for the upper and lower part of the toe are on separate needles. To prevent a hard, uncomfortable joining across the top of the toes, graft the stitches from the 2 needles together (see Volume 8, page 41.)

15 This finished sock is a classic shape with the K1, P1 ribbed top turned completely down onto the right side. As the sock has been made almost entirely in rounds, there is virtually no finishing to complete.

Mike Berend

Children's socks

Practice with the ribbed socks; then make the Argylls.

Ribbed socks

Sizes

To fit foot length, $6\frac{1}{4}[7\frac{1}{2}:8\frac{3}{4}]$in (16[19:22]cm).

Leg length to bottom of heel, $9\frac{1}{2}[11\frac{3}{4}:14\frac{1}{4}]$in (24[30:36]cm) with top turned back.

Note: Directions for larger sizes are in brackets []; if there is only one set of figures it applies to all sizes.

Materials

3[4:4]oz (60[80:80]g) of a sport yarn in main color (A)
Small amounts in each of 2 contrasting colors (B and C)
Set of four No. 2 (2¾mm) double-pointed knitting needles

Gauge

32 sts and 42 rows to 4in (10cm) in stockinette st on No. 2 (2¾mm) needles.

To make

Using set of four No. 2 (2¾mm) needles and A, cast on 52[60:68] sts and join into a round. Work 4 rounds K1, P1 ribbing. Cont in stockinette st (every round K), working in stripe sequence of 3[3:4] rounds A, 3[4:4] rounds B, 2[2:3] rounds A, 3[4:4] rounds C, 2[2:3] rounds A, 3[4:4] rounds B and 3[3:4] rounds A. Using A only cont in K1, P1 ribbing for $\frac{3}{4}[1:1\frac{1}{4}]$in (2[2.5:3]cm); end at end of a round. Turn work inside out to reverse turn-over top. Cont in rounds of K2, P2 ribbing until work measures 7[9:11]in (18[23:28]cm) from where work was reversed; end at end of a round.

Divide for heel

K14[16:18], then sl last 12[14:16] sts of round onto other end of same needle. Divide rem 26[30:34] sts onto 2 needles and leave for instep. Work $2\frac{1}{4}[2\frac{3}{4}:3\frac{1}{4}]$in (6[7:8]cm) stockinette st on heel sts; end with a P row.

Turn heel

1st row K14[16:18], sl 1, K1, psso, turn.
2nd row Sl 1, P2, P2 tog, turn.
3rd row Sl 1, K3, sl 1, K1 psso, turn.
4th row Sl 1, P4, P2 tog, turn.
Cont in this way, working one more st on every row, until all sts are worked; end with a P row. 14[16:18] sts.
Next row K7[8:9]. This completes heel. Sl instep sts back onto one needle. With spare needle, K7[8:9], pick up and K15[16:17] sts up side of heel; with 2nd needle, rib across instep sts; with 3rd needle, pick up and K15[16:17] sts down side of heel, then K7[8:9]. 70[78:86] sts.
Next round On first and 3rd needles, K to end; on 2nd needle, work in ribbing.
Next round On first needle, K to last 3 sts,

K2 tog, K1; on 2nd needle, rib to end; on 3rd needle, K1, sl 1, K1, psso K to end. Rep last 2 rounds until 50[58:66] sts rem. Cont straight until foot measures $4\frac{3}{4}[5\frac{1}{2}:6\frac{1}{2}]$in (12[14:16]cm) from back of heel; end at end of a round.

Shape toe

1st round On first needle, K to last 2 sts, K2 tog; on 2nd needle, K1, sl 1, K1, psso K to last 3 sts, K2 tog, K1; on 3rd needle, sl 1, K1, psso, K to end.
2nd round K to end.
Rep last 2 rounds until 18 sts rem; end with a first round. K sts from first needle onto 3rd needle and graft sts. Work a second sock in the same way.

Argyll pattern socks

Size

To fit foot length, $7\frac{1}{2}$in (19cm).
Leg length to bottom of heel, $12\frac{1}{2}$in (32cm).

Materials

2oz (40g) of a sport yarn in main color (A)
2oz (40g) each in contrasting colors (B and C)
Set of four No. 2 (2¾mm) double-pointed knitting needles

Gauge

32 sts and 42 rows to 4in (10cm) in plain stockinette st on No. 2 (2¾mm) needles.

To make

Using set of four No. 2 (2¾mm) needles and C, cast on 60 sts and join into a round. Work 6 rounds K1, P1 ribbing. Cont in stockinette st (every round K), working in patt from chart, reading every round from right to left, until work measures $2\frac{3}{4}$in (7cm); end at end of a round.

Shape leg

Next round K1, K2 tog, K to last 2 sts, K2 tog tbl.
Keeping patt correct at each side of shaping, cont to dec on every 6th round until 48 sts rem. Cont straight until work measures 10in (25cm); end at end of a round.

Divide for heel

Using C, K12, then sl last 11 sts of round onto other end of same needle. Divide rem 25 sts onto 2 needles and leave for instep. Work $2\frac{3}{4}$in (7cm) in rows of stockinette st on heel sts; end with a P row.

Turn heel

1st row K14, K2 tog tbl, turn.
2nd row P6, P2 tog, turn.
3rd row K6, K2 tog tbl, turn.
Rep 2nd and 3rd rows 6 times more, then work 2nd row again. 7 sts. Cut off yarn. Using C and with RS facing, pick up and K 21 sts down one side of heel, K the 7 sts, then pick up and K 21 sts up other side of heel. 49 sts.

Simon Butcher

Next row P to end.
Next row K1, K2 tog tbl, K to last 3 sts, K2 tog, K1.
Rep last 2 rows until 25 sts rem. Using C, cont straight until foot measures 6in (15cm) from back of heel; end with a P row. Leave these sts, but do not cut off yarn. Return to instep sts and sl them back onto one needle. Beg with RS row, cont in patt, inc one st at each end of first row. 27 sts. Cont straight until work measures same as under part of foot; end with a P row. Cut off yarns.

Toe

Using C, K the foot sts, then sts from upper part of foot. Divide these 52 sts onto 3 needles. Cont in rounds in C.
Next round Beg with foot sts, K1, K2 tog tbl, K19, K2 tog, K3, K2 tog tbl, K19, K2 tog, K2.
Next round K to end.
Next round K1, K2 tog tbl, K17, K2 tog, K3, K2 tog tbl, K17, K2 tog, K2.
Cont to dec in this way on every alternate round until 16 sts rem. Re-arrange sts onto 2 needles and graft sts.
Work a second sock in the same way.

To finish

Press or block according to yarn used. Join side seams of foot. Press seams.

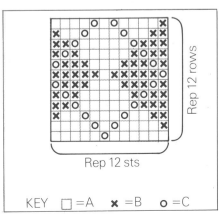

KEY □ =A   ✗ =B   ○ =C

Rep 12 rows

Rep 12 sts

John Hutchinson

Knitting / COURSE 72

*Mending knitting
*Reinforcing worn knitting
*Mending holes
*Stitch Wise: embossed
  stitches
*Pattern for a woman's
  sweater

Mending knitting

The custom of mending knitting is a dying one which is worth reviving. Earlier in the century mending was a matter of course and a darning box or basket was found in every household. Designers of knitting realized that garments would wear unevenly, and so designed them with this in mind. Sleeves were knitted in rounds so that if necessary whole sleeves or merely cuffs could be unraveled easily and re-knitted with no seams to impede the process. The heels and toes of socks were constructed for easy replacement. Before throwing away what you may think is a tattered old sweater—especially if it is a hand knit—stop to think of the ways to mend or remodel it. In this course are step-by-step instructions for reinforcing worn patches and for mending holes in knitting. On the right we show a selection of aids which you may find useful.

Reinforcing worn knitting

It is always a good idea to catch a worn patch on your knitted garment before it creates a hole. After all, mending holes is a much more difficult process than reinforcing thin areas with duplicate stitch (for detailed instructions on duplicate stitch see Volume 2, page 38). You will have to use your best judgment when

deciding what yarn to use for the repair. As you do not want the reinforcing to make the patch too thick, it is usually better to darn with a slightly thinner yarn than that of the garment. But if the area is very thin, you may find it necessary to use a yarn of the same weight as the garment. As for matching the color, remember that you

need not hide your repair but can make a decorative feature of it. Instead of covering the area with a simple square, triangle, diamond or heart shape in a contrasting color, you could be more creative and find a suitable figurative pattern, in a cross stitch or needlepoint book, for example, or on some printed fabric or wallpaper.

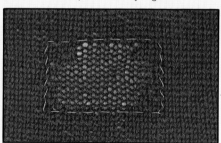

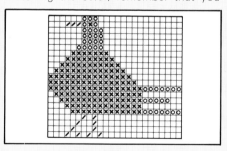

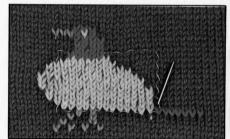

1 Before beginning the duplicate stitch, count the number of rows and stitches that are worn. Then calculate how many stitches need to be worked over in order to cover the thin area and overlap onto the stronger surrounding knitting so that the worn patch is strengthened.

2 Work out your own design or find a charted design that is big enough to cover the worn area.

3 Using a tapestry needle, work duplicate stitch slowly and carefully, especially over the very worn parts, so as not to tear the old yarn.

Mending holes

There are two traditional methods of repairing small holes in stockinette stitch. In the vertical method (steps 1-8), replacement stitches identical to knitted stitches, are worked over a base of vertical bars. In the horizontal method (lower right), stem stitch is worked over a base of horizontal bars. Although in this second method the stem stitches resemble a tightly worked stockinette stitch, they would not be suitable for a loosely knitted fabric and are not as strong or as durable as the stitches used in the first method. Try to match the yarn you use for the hole as closely as possible to the yarn of the garment being mended. Use a tapestry needle that is thin enough to pass easily through the loops.

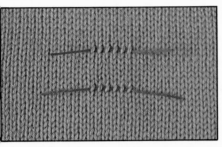

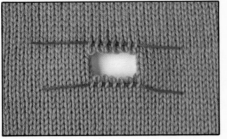

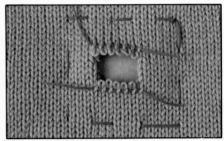

1 First run a strong fine cotton thread through each stitch in the rows that are completely intact at the top and bottom of the hole. These strands prevent further unraveling and can be pulled out once the vertical loops are in place.

2 Cut away the loose and damaged threads. Then unravel the last few loops at the top and bottom of the sides so that a few stitches can be folded to the back. Sew the folded sides securely to the back of the work.

3 Before beginning the darning, pin or baste the knitting to a thin piece of cardboard, so that it will not be stretched out of shape during the repair. If you are mending a sock, put it on a darning egg.

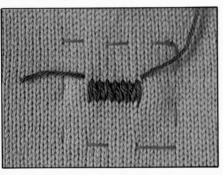

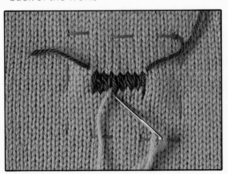

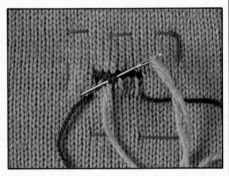

4 Secure a finer yarn of the same color (here a contrasting shade) to the fabric. Work long, loose, vertical stitches across the hole into the top and bottom loops as if you were making long duplicate stitches. Overlap the edges of the knitting at each side with two vertical strands.

5 Now secure the darning yarn to the fabric and begin working new loops across the bottom of the hole from right to left over the new vertical strands and through the loose loops of the original knitting.

6 At the end of the first row of new loops, pass the needle up to the center of the stitch above and make the next row from left to right. You may find it easier to work this row if you turn the garment, as we have done here.

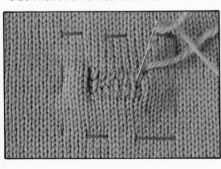

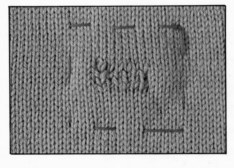

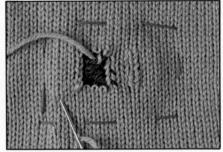

7 Continue making rows of new loops into the previous rows. In the last row catch up both the new loops and the loose loops of the original knitting at the top of the hole.

8 The repaired hole should be completely invisible. If it is a bit tight, this may be due to the vertical strands pulling the fabric up. These strands can be removed if desired.

9 To work horizontal base threads, first prepare as before, then work horizontal threads across the hole. Using darning yarn, work over base strands up and down vertically making stem stitches, as in embroidery. The first and last stitches in each row are worked into the loose loops at the top of the hole.

Fred Mancini

Stitch Wise

Embossed knitting

The following relief patterns are examples of embossed knitting. Like cables, the embossed shapes rise up like blisters from their sunken purl background. But unlike cable knitting, embossed textures are formed by increasing and decreasing units. They can be made into oval, diamond, circular or triangular shapes and are often used to imitate flames, berries,

bells, flowers or, as below, leaves.
All three patterns given here are written to be used as panels. Leaf eyelet stitch and fan leaf pattern are also very attractive as allover patterns. This is done by repeating the panels one after another. If you want to separate the panels with a knit stitch rib, remember, after calculating the number of stitches required for the panel repeats, to

add one stitch for every rib.
Elm leaf stitch is best used either as a single panel or with up to three repeats for a wider panel. It cannot be used as an allover pattern unless the leaf shapes are staggered, because the number of stitches in the row increases at the center of the leaf, which widens the fabric.

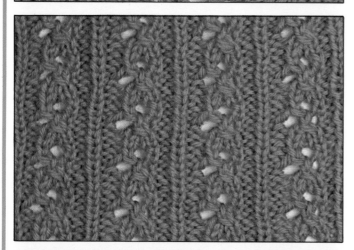

Fan leaf pattern

This pattern is worked over a panel of 22 sts.
1st and every other row (WS) P10, K2, P10.
2nd row K6, sl 1, K1, psso, return knit st to left-hand needle and with point of right-hand needle pass next st on left-hand needle over knit st and off needle, then sl the st back onto right-hand needle – called sl 1, K1, psso and pass –, yo, K1, yo, P2, yo, K1, yo, sl 1, K2 tog, psso, K6.
4th row K4, sl 1, K1, psso and pass, K1, (yo, K1) twice, P2, K1, (yo, K1) twice, sl 1, K2 tog, psso, K4.
6th row K2, sl 1, K1, psso and pass, K2, yo, K1, yo, K2, P2, K2, yo, K1, yo, K2, sl 1, K2 tog, psso, K2.
8th row Sl 1, K1, psso and pass, K3, yo, K1, yo, K3, P2, K3, yo, K1, yo, K3, sl 1, K2 tog, psso.
These 8 rows form the patt and are rep throughout.

Leaf eyelet stitch

This pattern is worked over a panel of 7 sts.
1st and every other row (WS) K2, P3, K2.
2nd row P2, yo, sl 1, K2 tog, psso, yo, P2.
4th row P2, K1, yo, sl 1, K1, psso, P2.
6th row P2, K3, P2.
These 6 rows form the patt and are rep throughout.

Elm leaf stitch

This pattern is worked over a panel of 7 sts.
1st row (WS) K to end.
2nd row P to end.
3rd row K to end.
4th row P3, K1, P3.
5th row K3, P into front, back and front again of next st, K3.
6th row P3, K3, P3.
7th row K3, P into front and back of next st, P1, P into front and back of next st, K3.
8th row P3, K5, P3.
9th row K3, P into front and back of next st, P3, P into front and back of next st, K3.
10th row P3, K7, P3.
11th row K3, P into front and back of next st, P5, P into front and back of next st, K3.
12th row P3, K9, P3.
13th row K3, P2 tog, P5, P2 tog tbl, K3.
14th row P3, K7, P3.
15th row K3, P2 tog, P3, P2 tog tbl, K3.
16th row P3, K5, P3.
17th row K3, P2 tog, P1, P2 tog tbl, K3.
18th row P3, K3, P3.
19th row K3, P3 tog, K3.
20th row P3, K1, P3.
These 20 rows form the patt and are rep throughout.

Woman's embossed sweater

Wear this lovely sweater in a warm tweedy yarn with your favorite casual clothes. The embossed panel is not hard to knit.

Sizes
To fit 32[34:36:38]in (83[87:92:97]cm) bust.
Length, 23¾[24¼:24¾:25½]in (60[61:63:64]cm).
Sleeve seam, 21¾in (54cm).
Note: Directions for larger sizes are in brackets []; if there is only one set of figures it applies to all sizes.

Materials
16[16:18:20]oz (450[450:500:550]g) of a knitting worsted (tweed-look yarn used here)
1 pair each Nos. 3 and 6 (3¼ and 4½mm) knitting needles
No. 6 (4½mm) circular knitting needle
Set of four No. 3 (3¼mm) double-pointed needles

Gauge
20 sts and 26 rows to 4in (10cm) in stockinette st on No. 6 (4½mm) needles.

Pattern panel
This panel is over 26 sts, but number of sts varies on different rows.
1st row P7, P2 tog, K into front and back of next st—called Kfb—, K2, P4, K2, yo, K1, yo, K2, P5.
2nd row K5, P7, K4, P2, K1, P1, K8.
3rd row P6, P2 tog, K1, P into front and back of next st—called Pfb—, K2, P4, K3, yo, K1, yo, K3, P5.
4th row K5, P9, K4, P2, K2, P1, K7.
5th row P5, P2 tog, K1, Pfb, P1, K2, P4,

Peter Waldman

37

sl 1, K1, psso, K5, K2 tog, P5.
6th row K5, P7, K4, P2, K3, P1, K6.
7th row P4, P2 tog, K1, Pfb, P2, K2, P4, sl 1, K1, psso, K3, K2 tog, P5.
8th row K5, P5, K4, P2, K4, P1, K5.
9th row P5, yo, K1, yo, P4, K2, P4, sl 1, K1, psso, K1, K2 tog, P5.
10th row K5, P3, K4, P2, K4, P3, K5.
11th row P5, (K1, yo) twice, K1, P4, K1, pick up loop lying between needles and K tbl – called make 1 (M1) –, K1, P2 tog, P2, sl 2 tog Knitwise, K1, p2sso, P5.
12th row K9, P3, K4, P5, K5.
13th row P5, K2, yo, K1, yo, K2, P4, K1, Kfb, K1, P2 tog, P7.
14th row K8, P1, K1, P2, K4, P7, K5.
15th row P5, K3, yo, K1, yo, K3, P4, K2, Pfb, K1, P2 tog, P6.
16th row K7, P1, K2, P2, K4, P9, K5.
17th row P5, sl 1, K1, psso, K5, K2 tog, P4, K2, P1, Pfb, K1, P2 tog, P5.
18th row K6, P1, K3, P2, K4, P7, K5.
19th row P5, sl 1, K1, psso, K3, K2 tog, P4, K2, P2, Pfb, K1, P2 tog, P4.
20th row K5, P1, K4, P2, K4, P5, K5.
21st row P5, sl 1, K1, psso, K1, K2 tog, P4, K2, P4, yo, K1, yo, P5.
22nd row K5, P3, K4, P2, K4, P3, K5.
23rd row P5, sl 2 tog Knitwise, K1, p2sso, P2, Ps tog, K1, M1, K1, P4, (K1, yo) twice, K1, P5.
24th row K5, P5, K4, P3, K9.

Back
Using No. 3 (3¼mm) needles cast on 90[94:102:106] sts.
1st and 4th sizes only
1st row P2, *K2, P2, rep from * to end.
2nd and 3rd sizes only
1st row K2, *P2, K2, rep from * to end.
All sizes
2nd row As first row, reading K for P and P for K.
Rep last 2 rows for 4in (10cm); end with a 2nd row and inc one st at each end of last row on 2nd and 4th sizes only.
90[96:102:108] sts. Change to No. 6 (4½mm) needles. **Beg with a P row, cont in reverse stockinette st, work 72 rows.
Shape armholes
Bind off 3 sts at beg of next 2 rows. Leave sts on holder.

Front
Work as back to **. Beg patt.
1st row P2[5:8:11], K2, (patt 26, K2) 3 times, P2[5:8:11].
2nd row K2[5:8:11], P2, (patt 26, P2) 3 times, K2[5:8:11].
Rep these 2 rows until 72 rows in all have been worked (3 complete patt repeats).
Shape armholes
Bind off 3 sts at beg of next 2 rows, working in patt on center 30 sts only. Leave sts on holder.

Sleeves
Using No. 3 (3¼mm) needles cast on 44[48:52:56] sts. Beg first row with K2, work in K2, P2 ribbing for 3¼in (8cm);

with a first row. Change to No. 6 (4½mm) needles. Beg patt.
1st row P7[9:11:13], K2, patt 26, K2, P7[9:11:13].
2nd row K7[9:11:13], P2, patt 26, P2, K7[9:11:13].
Cont in patt as set, inc one st at each end of 7th and every foll 8th row, working extra sts into reverse stockinette st, until there are 70[74:78:82] sts. Cont straight until 120 rows in all have been worked (5 complete patt repeats).
Shape top
Still working in patt, bind off 3 sts at beg of next 2 rows. Leave sts on holder.

Yoke
Using No. 6 (4½mm) circular needle and with RS facing, beg with sts of back, sl 1, K1, psso, P to last 2 sts, K2 tog, cont across first sleeve sl 1, K1, psso, patt to last 2 sts, K2 tog, cont across front, dec at each end in same way and working center 30 sts only in patt, then cont across second sleeve, dec in same way. 288[308:328:348] sts.
Next round Work in patt on sleeves and center front and reverse stockinette st on back, K2 at each "raglan seam".
Next round *Sl 1, K1, psso, work to next seam, K2 tog, rep from * to end.
Rep last 2 rounds until 24 rows of patt have been completed. Working all sts except seam sts in reverse stockinette st, cont to dec until 184[204:216:236] sts rem; end with a dec round.
Divide for neck
Sl the sts around needle until 2 center front sts are at point of needle, then sl these 2 sts onto a thread; with WS of work facing, rejoin yarn at left front neck and K to end, working P2 at each seam,

turn and cont in rows.
Next row P1, P2 tog, dec at each seam as before, work to last 3 sts, P2 tog tbl, P1. Cont to dec at neck edge on every 3rd row (on WS rows, K1, K2 tog tbl . . . K2 tog, K1) until 10[11:12:13] sts have been dec at each side of neck, *at the same time* cont to dec at each seam on every other row until 42[44:46:48] sts rem; end with a WS row.

Neckband
Using set of four No. 3 (3¼mm) needles and with RS facing, K across all sts on needle, pick up and K 30[33:34:37] sts down left front neck, K 2 center front sts, then pick up and K 30[33:34:37] sts up right front neck. 104[112:116:124] sts.
Next round Work in K2, P2 ribbing, work to one st before 2 center front sts, K2 tog, sl 1, K1, psso, rib to end.
Rep last round for 1¼in (3cm). Bind off in ribbing, dec at center front.

To finish
Press or block pieces according to yarn used. Join side and sleeve seams. Press seams.

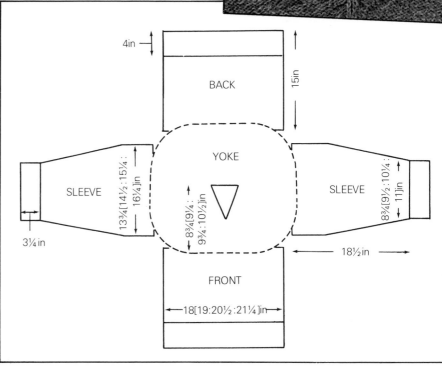

*More ideas for remodeling
 knitting
*Replacing ribbing
*Adding fabric trimmings to
 knitting
*Pattern for a girl's party dress
 and jumper with
 fabric insert

More ideas for remodeling knitting

You may want to alter a knitted garment to bring it up to date or to refit it to a growing child. In Volume 11, page 49 detailed instructions for lengthening your knitting are given, and the pattern in Volume 11, page 52 shows how to incorporate stripes. When facing a knitting repair job, think of it as an opportunity to give a completely new look to the garment.

This need not mean hours of work, since even the smallest detail can transform a dreary old sweater. All you need is patience and care in choosing the right color to complement the existing knitting. The parts of a sweater that are most often in need of repair are the elbows and the ribbing around the cuffs, neck and armholes. Ribbings are easily replaced

and it is worth the effort. Sleeves can be removed or shortened and bound with fabric to eliminate unsightly holes at the elbow. Next time you see a hand-knitted wool sweater at a garage sale that is frayed at the edges or much too short, but otherwise wearable, think of how you could transform it with a few hours of work.

Replacing ribbing

If the ribbing on a sweater is discolored or damaged, you can give a new look to the garment by replacing it, using a contrasting color. Do not underestimate the difference that even the replacement of the last few rows of the ribbing can make

to the overall appearance of a sweater. You may like to try removing all of the ribbing at the neck, waistband and cuffs and replacing them with a cable stitch. In either case you should first make a gauge sample to decide what needle size to use.

For the cabled ribbing you will also have to determine how many stitches are needed in the row to suit the pattern. The instructions show a cuff being altered, but any ribbing section can be treated in the same way.

Adding a stripe at the edge of the ribbing

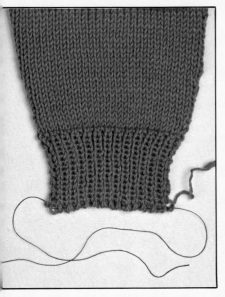
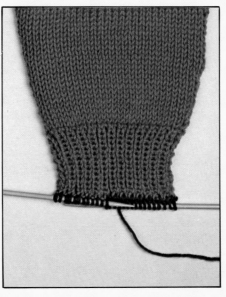

1 If only the edge of the ribbing is damaged you need only replace the last few rows. First unpick the side seam. Then run a strong fine thread through a row that is still intact, close to the edge, and unravel up to this row.

2 Pick the stitches up on the knitting needle. Once all the loops are on the needle, pull out the cotton thread. Then, using a contrasting yarn, work a few rows in ribbing.

3 Bind off the stitches loosely and sew up the seam again. You may find that repeating the edging on another ribbed part of the garment gives this detail a more coordinated look.

Adding cabled ribbing

1 Unpick the seam and run a strong thread through the first row outside the ribbing. Then unravel the ribbing and adjust the length of stockinette stitch.

2 Pick up the stitches and pull out the thread. Using a contrasting color, begin the cabled ribbing. In the first row adjust the number of stitches if necessary.

3 Work the new ribbing to the required length. Then bind off loosely. A cable ribbing is suitable for a turtleneck or cuffs.

Adding fabric trimmings to knitting

You may not want to—or be unable to—spend time re-knitting trimmings for your worn garments. In this case, fabric trimmings are the answer. Bound fabric edging can be used to replace ribbing, and fabric insertions can be used to lengthen skirts or sleeves. Choose a fabric of a suitable weight—medium-weight wool for a thick sweater or fine cotton fo fine knits. Sew on the trimming by hand or, if you have a sewing machine, use a zig-zag stitch.

Binding armholes with fabric

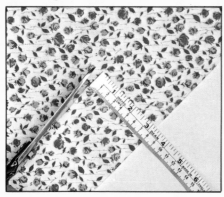

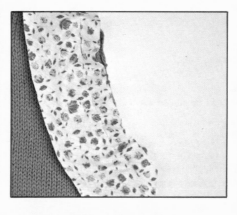

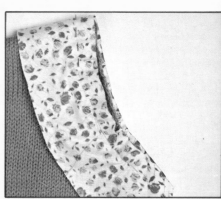

1 Prepare your garment by removing set-in sleeves or armhole ribbing. Then cut bias fabric strips four times width of finished band—3in (8cm)-wide strips for a ¾in (2cm)-wide band.

2 The length of the strip should be the distance around the armhole plus seam allowances. Pin the fabric to the knitting, right sides together and edges matching. Start at the underarm seam.

3 Make sure the fabric is not puckered and is stretched out around the curves. Using thread suited to the fabric and yarn, make small even running stitches around the armhole ¾in (2cm) from the edge.

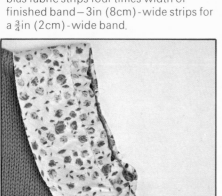

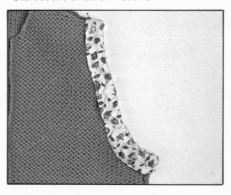

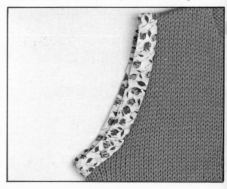

4 Where the ends meet under the arm sew the strip together; trim the seam and press it open.

5 Fold the binding over the edge to the underside and turn under ¾in (2cm). Pin the binding in place and slip stitch.

6 The bias trimming gives a neat edge to the armhole and would look equally attractive added around a wide neck.

Lengthening a skirt with a fabric insertion

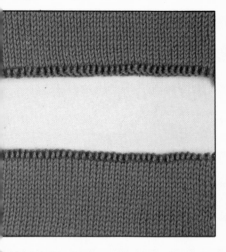

1 Unpick the side seams and separate the hem section from the top of the skirt (see Volume 11, pages 49-50). Make sure the hem section is deep enough to give a good weight to the bottom of the skirt.

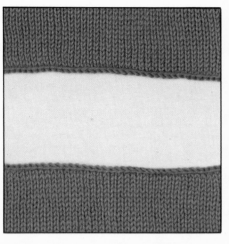

2 Pick up the stitches of each of the four sections and bind off the edges with separate lengths of yarn.

3 Lay the top of the front of the skirt and the knitted hem onto a piece of pattern paper, leaving the desired gap between them. Trace the shape of the space between the two sections.

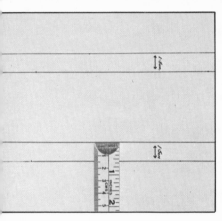

4 Cut out the paper pattern, allowing at least a ½in (1.2cm) seam allowance all the way around. Use the same pattern for the back if it is identical to the front.

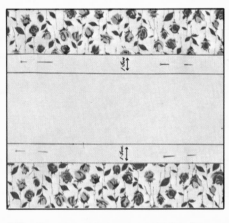

5 Pin the paper pattern onto the fabric perpendicular to the selvage and cut two pieces.

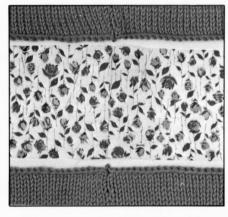

6 Stitch the insertions together at the sides. Then stitch the front and back tops of the skirt and the two hem sections together again at the sides.

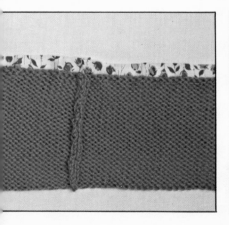

7 Lining up the side seams, pin the lower edge of the insertion to the hem of the skirt with right sides facing. The bound-off edge of the knitting should fall just above the fabric seamline.

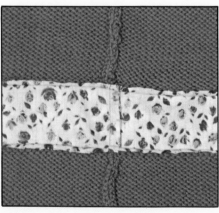

8 Back stitch the fabric and the knitting together just below the bound-off edge. Then secure the upper edge of the fabric insertion to the top of the skirt in the same way.

9 After completion press the skirt gently as appropriate for the fibers. If the skirt is going to be washed frequently or if the fabric frays easily you may want to finish the fabric seam allowances.

Girl's party dress and jumper with fabric insert

Two dresses for the price of one! A ruffled party dress can be easily converted into a pretty jumper if you follow our instructions. And the fabric is reversible, too.

Stuart Macleod

When your child grows out of the party dress, don't throw it away. Instead make a jumper: remove the sleeves and neck ruffle, bind the armhole and neck edge and insert a strip of fabric above the lower ruffle.

Party dress

Sizes
To fit 22[24]in (56[61]cm) chest. Length, 17¾[20½]in (46[53]cm), including ruffle. Sleeve seam, 9½[10¾]in (24[27]cm), including ruffle.
Note Directions for the larger size are in brackets []; if there is only one set of figures it applies to both sizes.

Materials
13[15]oz (350[400]g) of a knitting worsted
1 pair each Nos. 3 and 5 (3¼ and 4mm) knitting needles
1yd (1m) of narrow ribbon

Gauge
20 sts and about 44 rows to 4in (10cm) in patt on No. 5 (4mm) needles.

Back
Using No. 5 (4mm) needles cast on 75[85] sts.
1st row (RS) P1, *yarn to back, sl 1 purlwise, yarn to front, P1, rep from * to end.
2nd row P to end.
3rd row P2, *yarn to back, sl 1 purlwise, yarn to front, P1, rep from * to last st, P1.
4th row P to end.
These 4 rows form patt. Rep them throughout. Work 4 more rows. Dec one st at each end of next and every foll 12th row until 59[67] sts rem. Cont straight until work measures 10¾(12¼]in (27[31]cm); end with a WS row.
Shape armholes
Bind off 4 sts at beg of next 2 rows. Dec one st at each end of next and foll alternate row, then every 4th row 2[3] times more. 43[49] sts. Cont straight until armholes measure 4¾[5½]in (12[14]cm); end with a WS row.
Shape neck and shoulders
1st row Patt 14[16], turn and leave rem sts on a spare needle.
2nd row Bind off 2 sts, patt to end.
3rd row Bind off 34 sts, patt to end.
Rep 2nd and 3rd rows once more. Work 1 row. Bind off rem 4 sts.
With RS facing, rejoin yarn to rem sts on spare needle, bind off 15[17] sts, patt to end.
Next row Bind off 34 sts, patt to end.
Next row Bind off 2 sts, patt to end. Rep last 2 rows once more. Bind off rem 4 sts.

Front
Work as for back to completion of armhole shaping. 43[49] sts. Cont straight until armholes measure 2¼[2¾]in (6[7]cm); end with a WS row.
Shape neck
Next row Patt 16[18], turn and leave rem sts on a spare needle.
Bind off 2 sts at beg of next row. Dec one st at neck edge on foll 4 alternate rows. 10[12] sts. Cont straight until armhole measures same as back to shoulder; end at armhole edge with a P row.
Shape shoulder
Bind off 3[4] sts at beg of next and foll alternate row. Work 1 row. Bind off rem 4 sts. With RS facing, rejoin yarn to rem sts on spare needle, bind off 11[13] sts, patt to end. Complete as first side.

Lower edge ruffle (make 2 pieces)
Using No. 3 (3¼mm) needles cast on 113[117] sts. K 3 rows. Change to No. 5 (4mm) needles. P 1 row. Work 2¾[3¼]in (7[8]cm) patt as for back; end with a RS row. Bind off.

Neck ruffle
Using No. 3 (3¼mm) needles cast on 121[137] sts. Work as for lower edge ruffle until work measures 2[2¼]in; end with a RS row. Change to No. 5 (4mm) needles. K 1 row.
Next row K2, *yo, K2 tog, K2, rep from * to last 3 sts, yo, K2 tog, K1. K 2 rows. Bind off knitwise.

Sleeves
Using No. 3 (3¼mm) needles cast on 39[43] sts. K 3 rows. Change to No. 5 (4mm) needles. P 1 row. Cont in patt as for back until work measures 9½[10¾]in (24[27]cm); end with a WS row.
Shape top
Bind off 4 sts at beg of next 2 rows. Dec one st at each end of next and every foll 4th row 4 times more, then every other row 5 times; end with a WS row. Bind off 2 sts at beg of next 2[4] rows. Bind off rem 7 sts.

To finish
Press or block, according to yarn used. Join shoulder seams. Join side and sleeve seams. Join seams of lower edge ruffle, gather and sew in place. Join seam of neck ruffle, gather and sew to neck edge with seam at center back. Thread ribbon through holes at neck. Run a gathering thread, or narrow elastic, through sleeve at wrist level, leaving about 1½in (4cm) below gathers to form ruffle. Press seams.

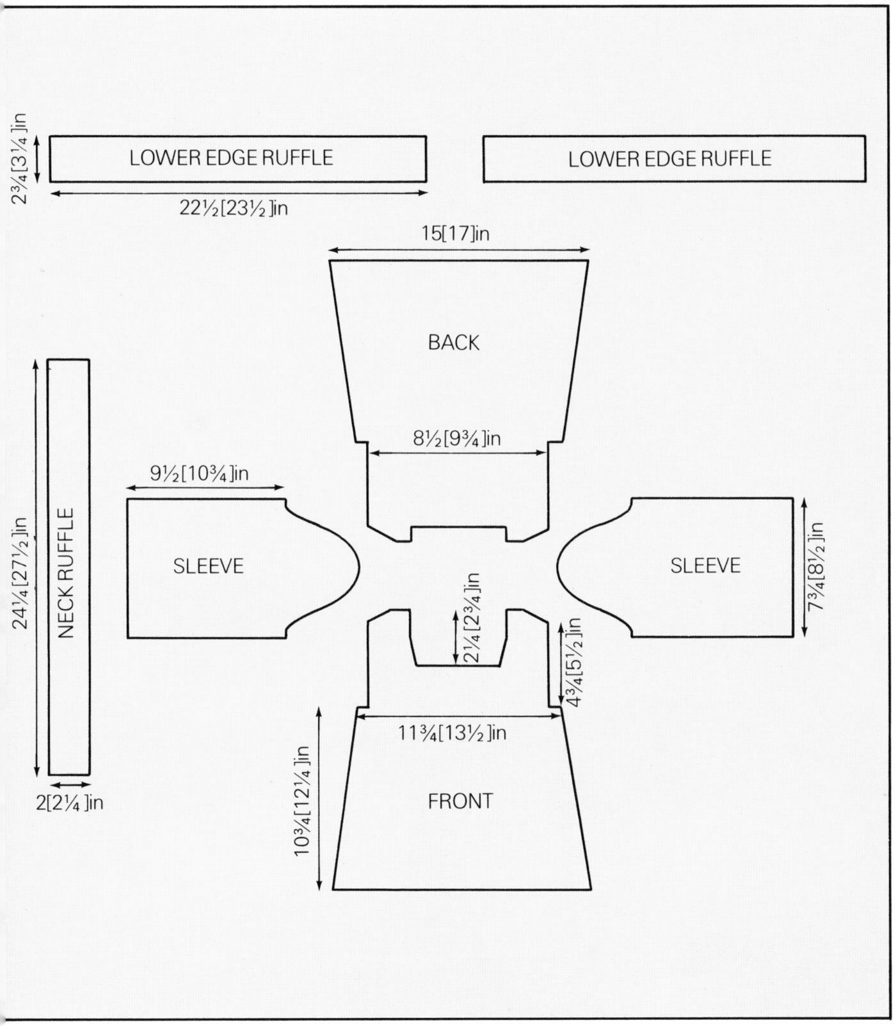

LOWER EDGE RUFFLE — LOWER EDGE RUFFLE — 2¾[3¼]in — 22½[23½]in
BACK — 15[17]in — 8½[9¾]in
NECK RUFFLE — 24¼[27]in — 2[2¼]in
SLEEVE 9½[10¾]in — SLEEVE 7¾[8½]in
FRONT — 11¾[13½]in — 2¼[2¾]in — 4¾[5½]in — 10¾[12¼]in

43

Jumper

Sizes
To fit 22[24]in (56[61]cm) chest.
Length, 18¼[21]in (46[53]cm) **plus**
required depth of fabric insert.
Note Directions for the larger size are
in brackets []; if there is only one set of
figures it applies to both sizes.

Materials
  9[11]oz (250[300]g) of a knitting
    worsted
  1 pair each Nos. 3 and 5 (3¼ and
    4mm) knitting needles

About ½yd (.5m) of 36in (90cm)-
wide fabric

Gauge
20 sts and about 44 rows to 4in (10cm) in
patt on No. 5 (4mm) needles.

Back, front and lower edge ruffle
Work as for party dress.

To finish
Press or block, according to yarn used.
Join shoulder seams.
Fabric insertion Following steps of
"Lengthening with fabric insertions,"
page 41 as a guide, cut 2 pieces of
fabric to fit in between lower edges of
front and back skirt and ruffle (remember
to continue shape of side edges of skirt
onto fabric). Sew fabric in place at lower
edge of skirt. Join side seams.
Armhole edging Cut two 1½in (4cm)-
wide bias strips to fit armhole. See
"Binding armholes with fabric" on page
40 for steps on how to apply edging.
Neck edging Cut 1½in (4cm)-wide bias
strip of fabric, to fit neck edge. Proceed as
for armhole edging.
Join seams of lower edge ruffle, gather
and sew in place. Press seams.

Shoestring

Restful bath

This small pillow, made from fabric remnants, will cushion your head in the bathtub without getting damaged by the water.

Finished size
11 × 9in (28 × 23cm) (excluding ruffle).
A seam allowance of ½in (1cm) is included.

Materials
> ½yd (.5m) of 36in (90cm)-wide
> cotton or cotton/polyester
> ⅜yd (.3m) of 36in (90cm)-wide
> lightweight plastic fabric
> Washable stuffing
> Matching thread
> Two plastic hooks with self-adhesive
> backs
> Tailor's chalk

1 Cut two strips of cotton fabric, 36 × 4in (90 × 10cm). Fold strips in half along length, wrong sides together. Mark the center of each long raw edge with tailor's chalk. Open out strips again.
2 With right sides facing and raw edges matching, pin and stitch ends of strips together to form a ring. Press seams open. Fold strip in half again.
3 Cut a 10in (25cm) strip of fabric across the fabric width. Divide this strip into: one piece 12 × 10in (30 × 25cm) for pillow front; two pieces for pillow back— 12 × 10in (30 × 25cm) and 10 × 5in (25 × 12cm); and two pieces 10 × 2in (25 × 5cm) for hanging loops.

4 Fold one loop in half lengthwise, right sides together. Pin and stitch ½in (1cm) from raw edges down length of strip. Turn strip right side out and press it with the seam lying in the center.
5 Repeat step 4 to make other hanging loop in the same way.
6 Run a line of gathering stitches through the long raw edges of the ruffle, stitching through both layers.
7 Mark the center of each edge of pillow front.
8 Pull up gathering threads on ruffle. Pin ruffle to right side of pillow front, matching raw edges and placing the seams at the centers of the short sides and the ruffle chalk marks at the centers of the long sides. Adjust gathers evenly, baste in place and stitch.
9 Pin and baste both short ends of loops to one long edge of right side of pillow front, over ruffle, positioning them with seams on the inside, 3¼in (8cm) from corners of pillow, with raw edges matching.
10 Turn under a ½in (1cm) double hem along one short side of the larger pillow back section. Turn under a ½in (1cm) double hem along one 10in (25cm) edge of the smaller pillow back section.
11 Place the larger of the pillow back

sections on the pillow front with right sides together and three raw edges matching. Place the smaller pillow back section over the larger back section so that the long raw edge of the smaller section matches the free raw edge of the pillow front.
12 Pin, baste and stitch around all four edges, catching in the ruffle and hanging loops as you stitch. Finish raw edges with zig-zag stitch. Clip corners. Turn pillowcase right side out.
13 For inner cover, cut a strip of plastic fabric 24 × 11in (60 × 27cm). Fold it in half with wrong sides facing to form a rectangle 12 × 11in (30 × 27cm). Join the two long sides, using a French seam and taking ½in (1cm) seam allowance each time. Turn inner cover right side out.
14 Stuff the inner cover. Turn under a ½in (1cm)-wide double hem across the open end.
Stitch hemmed edges together.
15 Slip into pillow cover.
16 Place the pillow on the edge of the bathtub in a comfortable position, as shown, with the loops extending behind it. Mark the positions for the hooks. Fix the hooks to the tub or to the tiled area around it, following the manufacturer's instructions.

* Working method for spool knitting
* Joining in a new ball of yarn or a different color
* Joining cord to form strips and a ring
* Pattern for a circular shoulder bag in spool knitting

Working method for spool knitting

There is a form of knitting in which gauge is unimportant, provided that you work neatly. Using a spool, rather than a pair of needles, you can make a type of 3-dimensional work known as spool or French knitting. Instead of a fabric, this technique produces a cord composed of rounds of four knitted stitches.

Spool knitting can form the basis of a fabric if the cords are sewn together. Used individually, lengths of cord make attractive trimmings such as cording or frog fastenings.

Alternatively, you can join the cord together in strips to form belts or bag handles; coiled into a circle and sewn together, the cord becomes a mat, rug or bag (see step-by-step pictures opposite); it can also be applied to an adhesive backing (see instructions for bag on page 48). The best yarn for spool knitting is a smooth sport yarn or knitting worsted, according to the thickness of cord you need. If the yarn is too hairy or textured, it will not travel smoothly through the hole in the spool.

1 This commercial spool and a tapestry needle are the only equipment you need for spool knitting. Basically the "knitter" is a wooden cylinder with a hole—up to ⅜in (1cm) in diameter—down through the center of it. The top has four equidistant staples around which the yarn is wound.

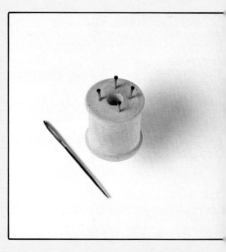

2 A homemade spool is just as suitable for spool knitting. It consists of an ordinary empty spool with four small nails or tacks (the small, flat "head" is useful to prevent the stitches from falling off) hammered at equal distances around the hole. Use a large tapestry needle or fine crochet hook for working the stitches.

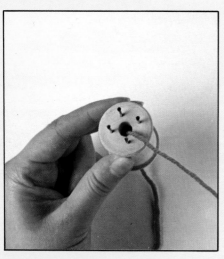

3 To start work, thread the end of a ball of yarn down through the spool so that it hangs free for about 4in (10cm) at the lower end. Hold the spool in your left hand while you are working.

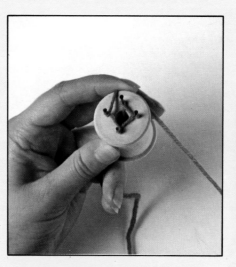

4 Holding the end of yarn at the lower edge in place with your left hand, wind the yarn at the top in a counter-clockwise direction around each peg in turn.

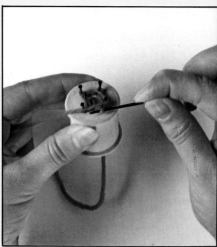

5 To make the stitches, work in a clockwise direction and bring the yarn around the outside of each peg in turn. Insert the needle into the bottom loop already on the peg and draw it up, over the yarn strand and the top loop and off the peg. Continue in rounds, working each stitch in the same way.

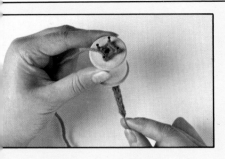

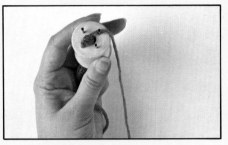

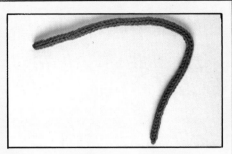

6 There is no need to mark your place if you put the work down; when starting off, always work the next stitch to the left of the yarn. As the knitting builds up on the pegs, clear them by gently pulling the end of yarn at the lower edge. The stitches disappear down the hole and gradually a cord appears at the lower edge.

7 When the cord is the desired length (remember to allow for length inside spool), finish by taking the loop where the yarn is and placing it on the next peg to the left: lift the lower loop over the top loop. Continue in this way until one loop remains. Cut yarn about 4in (10cm) from work, thread through last loop and pull up tightly.

8 Draw the finished cord out of the spool: it is a solid circular shape comprising 4 stitches in rounds with a smooth, stockinette stitch appearance.

Joining in a new ball of yarn or a different colour

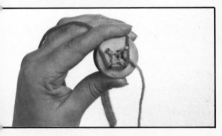

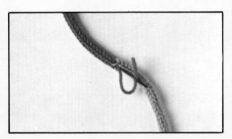

1 When about 4in (10cm) of the old ball of yarn remains, take the new ball of yarn or color and, leaving a 4in (10cm) end, simply wind it in a clockwise direction around the outside of the pegs.

2 Holding the new yarn in place with your left hand, continue to work the next and following stitches in the usual way with the new yarn or color. The last stitch in the old yarn may be loose; pull the old end of yarn to tighten it.

3 Keep the two ends of yarn clear as you are working and they will eventually be drawn down the hole. When the cord is complete, darn in the ends; feed them through the center of the cord away from the joining before trimming the ends. The color change looks very neat with little displacement of stitches.

Joining cord to form strips and a ring

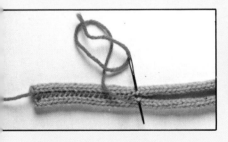

1 To join two lengths of cord together to form a strip, lay them side by side. Thread a tapestry needle with matching yarn (here it is contrasting color for clarity). Keep the stitches on both cords running in a straight line and overcast neighboring stitches on the two cords together.

2 The work is almost flat on the wrong side when the seaming is complete, but the right side still has a ridged, corded appearance. If you have not sewn along a straight line of stitches, the cords will have an unattractive, twisted look.

3 To make a circular fabric, attach the yarn to one coiled end and join it into a tight circle. Continue to overcast the cords together as you are winding the circle. Keep the line of stitches in the same place or they will become twisted. As the circle grows it is more difficult to keep it flat; sticking the spiral to an adhesive backing is a way of keeping a large circle flat.

Frederick Mancini

Circular shoulder bag in spool knitting

Work long lengths of spool knitting to make this versatile shoulder bag.

Size
Diameter of bag, about 8in (20cm).
Length from bottom of bag to shoulder, about 24in (60cm).

Materials
4oz (100g) of a knitting worsted in main color (A)
1oz (25g) in each of two contrasting colors (B and C)
Knitting spool
1 pair No. 5 (4mm) knitting needles
8in (20cm) zipper
⅜yd (.3m) each of iron-on interfacing, interlining, lining material and fusible webbing

To make
Using A, knit 2 lengths of spool knitting about 5½yd (5m) long, enough to coil into two 8in (20cm)-diameter circles for main part of bag. Knit 3 lengths, 1 in each color, about 60in (150cm) long, for strap. Knit 2 lengths, 1 in each of B and C, about 25½in (65cm) long, for trimming.

Gusset
Using No. 5 (4mm) needles and A, cast on 14 sts. Work 8¼in (21cm) stockinette st; end with a P row.
Next row K7, turn and leave rem sts on a safety pin.
Cont on first 7 sts for 8in (20cm); end with a K row. Leave sts on a safety pin. Rejoin yarn to sts that were left. Cont in stockinette st to match first side; end with a K row.
Next row P across both sets of sts.
Cont in stockinette st for a further 8¾in (22.5cm). Bind off.

To finish
Sides of bag Coil each length into a close spiral on a flat surface. Cut fusible webbing and interfacing to same size, then cut interlining and lining, allowing 1in (2.5cm) all around. Use fusible webbing to bond interlining and coiled circle, pressing down firmly. Secure coil permanently with several lines of hand stitches, worked outward from center on interlining side.

Iron on interfacing. Fold and press excess interlining all around on top of interfacing. Place lining on top. Snip and turn under raw edges all around. Pin and baste in place.
Gusset Sew zipper into opening. Cut interfacing to fit, making an opening around zipper, and iron on.
Cut lining with ½in (1.2cm) hem allowance: cut slit for zipper and snip the corners. Turn under hems, then pin and sew in place all around outer edge. Turn under and hem lining around zipper. Join short ends of gusset to form a ring.
Join gusset to sides of bag by overcasting from the outside, sewing through lining of sides of bag at same time. Trim outer edge of circle, covering the seam, with contrasting lengths of spool knitting.
Using A, make 4 short lengths of spool knitting to hold strap in place. Sew to gusset at regular intervals. Thread 3 lengths for straps through loops on gusset, then join each into a ring. Sew through the strands at intervals to prevent them from separating.

*Using spool knitting as cording
*Shape and color effects in spool knitting
*Pattern for a woman's sweater trimmed with cording

Using spool knitting as cording

Lengths of spool knitting make an ideal form of cording. The knitted cord is fairly solid, so there is no need to use a central core to give it "body" as with dressmaking or furnishing fabrics.

There are two main ways of using the cord. One method is to sew it on top of a flat seam when the garment is complete. Used in this way it accentuates raglans, armholes, front bands, patch pockets and collars.

The other method is to insert the cording into the seam so that it forms a trimming around the outer edge of the finished piece of knitting—for example, around the edge of a tea cozy or hat.

1 Join the seams of the knitted fabric in the usual way. If necessary, press the seams at this point. Make the cord to fit the length of the seam. Choose a color contrasting with the main fabric, or if the background is tweedy, pick one of the tweed colors to accentuate it.

2 As a guide for stitching the cord along a straight line, mark a horizontal line of half stitches with plenty of pins along the cord.

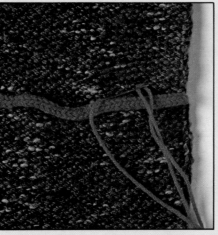

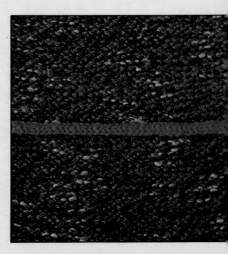

3 Place the cord one row below the finished seam on the right side of the fabric. Using the pins to mark a straight line, pin the cord in place—first at one end of the seam—one row below the seam. After sewing, the cord will roll over and hide the seam.

4 Using yarn matching the cord and a tapestry needle, slip stitch the cord in place along the seam. Be careful to work into a straight line of knitted stitches indicated by the pins.

5 The finished cord sits neatly in place, covering the seamline underneath. If you have sewn along a line of stitches, they will run in parallel lines; otherwise the lines of stitches will have a twisted, unsightly appearance.

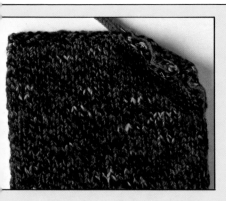

6 To insert a cord into a seam, with right sides of the two pieces of knitting facing, insert the cord between them along the edge to be piped. Pin the cord in place so that a straight, single chain of stitches is visible.

7 Using a tapestry needle threaded with yarn matching the cord, sew a backstitch seam close to the edge of the wrong side of the knitted fabric, working through all thicknesses. The line of cording stitches should remain visible.

8 On the right side of the completed fabric, the cord forms a trimming around the entire edge. The stitching is invisible where it is caught into the seam.

Shape and color effects in spool knitting

It is fun to experiment with spool knitting. It is best to use a plain, smooth yarn; the resulting cord is a smooth knit without any texture. Therefore, use colored yarns and different shapes to exploit this medium to its fullest potential.

In addition to the usual flat circular or rectangular shapes used for mats, you can make domed shapes, baskets and unusual abstract shapes for ornaments, key-ring tabs or even Christmas tree decorations.

This is a flat circle made from a single cord where the colors have been changed at random intervals (see "Joining in a new ball of yarn or a different color," page 47). Odds and ends of yarn are ideal for this as spool knitting uses very small quantities.

You can also make a rectangular or square shape out of short lengths of spool knitting. Simply make equal-size lengths of spool knitting and sew them together. Random shades of one color make an attractive pattern.

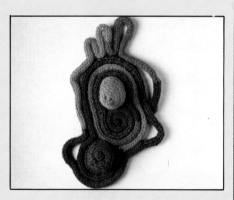

In addition to making flat, circular shapes, you can easily coil a length of cord into a domed shape similar to a beehive or sea shell. Instead of stitching the spiral in a flat plane, form the dome as you are sewing it; turn the work inside out on completion to hide the stitches. Make a flat circular shape as the base of a basket, then curve the sides.

Try making unusual free-form shapes based on a flat circle and using different colors. Break the regular spiraling of the cord simply by catching it together either with a single stitch to cause a small deflection or by doubling the cord back to make a large obstruction.

Even more complicated and adventurous free-form shapes can be made with the use of domed shapes to give a three-dimensional effect. Interrupt the coiling of the flat, circular shape by sewing the dome into the pattern, then continue coiling around the base of the dome.

Fred Mancini

Sweater trimmed with cording

This sweater illustrates just how effective spool knitting can be when it is used as cording on raglan seams, collar and neckline.

Chris Harvey

Sizes

To fit 34[36:38]in (87[92:97]cm) bust. Length, 25¾[26:26¾]in (65[66:68]cm). Sleeve seam, 12½in (32cm).

Note Directions for larger sizes are in brackets [ ]; if there is only one set of figures it applies to all sizes.

Materials

22[23:25]oz (600[650:700]g) of a knitting worsted (A)
2oz (50g) of a sport yarn for cording (B)
Nos. 6 and 8 (4½ and 5½mm) knitting needles
3 buttons
Knitting spool

Gauge

17 sts and 25 rows to 4in (10cm) in reverse stockinette st on No. 8 (5½mm) needles.

Back

Using No. 6 (4½mm) needles and A cast on 81[85:89] sts.
1st row K1, *P1, K1, rep from * to end.
2nd row P1, *K1, P1, rep from * to end.
Rep these 2 rows for 2¾in (7cm); end with a 2nd row.
Change to No. 8 (5½mm) needles. Beg with a P row, cont in reverse stockinette st until work measures 11½in (29cm); end with a K row.
Shape raglan
Cont in reverse stockinette st, dec one st at each end of next and every foll 4th row until 59[65:67] sts rem, then at each end of every foll 3rd row until 27[29:31] sts rem. Work 1 row. Bind off.

Front

Work as for back to raglan shaping; end with a K row.
Shape raglan
Dec one st at each end of next and every foll 4th row until 63[67:69] sts rem; end with a dec row. Work 1[3:3] rows.
Divide for front opening
1st size only
Next row P27, turn and leave rem sts on spare needle.
Complete left side of opening first.
Work 1 row. Dec one st at raglan edge on next and foll 4th row. 25 sts.
2nd and 3rd sizes only
Next row P2 tog, P27[28], turn and leave rem sts on spare needle.
Complete left side of opening first.
All sizes
Keeping opening edge straight, dec one st at raglan edge on every foll 3rd row until 12[13:14] sts rem; end with a dec row. Work 2[1:0] rows.
Shape neck
Cont to dec at raglan edge as before, dec one st at front edge on every row until 2 sts rem. Work 2 sts tog. Fasten off.
With RS facing, rejoin yarn to rem sts, bind off 9 sts for base of front opening, P to end, working 2 sts tog at end of row

on 2nd and 3rd sizes only. 27[28:29] sts. Complete to match other side of opening and neck.

Sleeves

Using No. 6 (4½mm) needles and A cast on 39[41:43] sts. Work 2in (5cm) ribbing as for back; end with a 2nd row. Change to No. 8 (5½mm) needles. Beg with a P row, work 2in (5cm) reverse stockinette st; end with a K row. Inc one st at each end of next and every foll 5th row until there are 61[63:65] sts. Work 5 more rows; end with a K row.
Shape raglan
Dec one st at each end of next and every foll 4th row until 39[43:37] sts rem, then at each end of every foll 3rd row until 7[7:9] sts rem. Work one row.
Bind off.

Collar

Using No. 6 (4½mm) needles and A cast on 41[43:47] sts for back neck. Work 2 rows K1, P1 ribbing as for back. Cont in ribbing, cast on 6 sts at beg of next 4 rows and 4 sts at beg of foll 2 rows. 73[75:79] sts. Cont in ribbing until collar measures 4in (10cm) at center back neck; end with a 2nd row. Bind off in ribbing.

Buttonhole band

Using No. 6 (4½mm) needles and A cast on 13 sts. Cont in K1, P1 ribbing as for back for 2¼in (6cm); end with a 2nd row.
1st buttonhole row Rib 5, bind off 3 sts, rib to end.
2nd buttonhole row Rib to end, casting on 3 sts over those bound off in last row. Cont in ribbing, making 2 more buttonholes at intervals of 2¼in (6cm) measured from base of last buttonhole. Rib 2 rows after last buttonholes. Bind off in ribbing.

Button band

Work to match buttonhole band, omitting buttonholes.

To finish

Press or block according to yarn used. Join raglan seams. Using B, make 4 lengths of spool knitting cord to fit along raglans. Sew in place. Sew button band in place down left side of front opening and along lower edge. Sew buttonhole band in place down right side of opening and overlapping button band at lower edge. Matching center back of collar to center back of garment, sew RS of collar to WS of neck, beg and ending at top of front opening. Using B, make another length of spool knitting to fit down left side of front opening, across lower edge, up right edge of opening and around entire edge of collar. Sew cord in place with seam at center back of collar.
Join side and sleeve seams.
Press seams.
Sew on buttons.

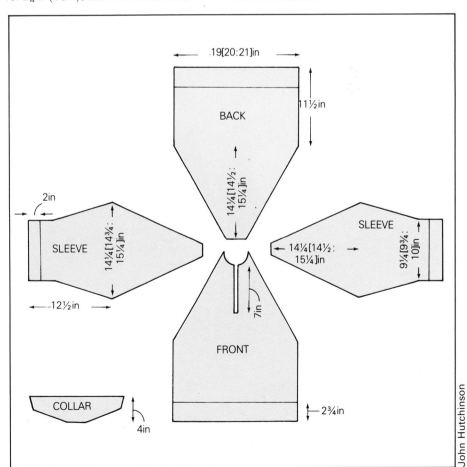

John Hutchinson

Sewing / COURSE 68

*Conspicuous bound seams
*Easy binding
*Pattern for an evening jacket
and bag: adapting the
pattern; directions
for making

Conspicuous bound seams

Conspicuous bound seams give an attractive design detail to seam finishes and are ideal for open-weave fabrics and fabrics which ravel easily. The seam is made on the right side; the seam allowance is bound and then stitched flat. Contrasting fabric or bias binding can be used to bind the seam. On the jacket on page 57 we have used gold fabric to coordinate with the gold mesh of the main fabric. When stitching net or other open fabrics, use tissue paper underneath and tear it away afterward.

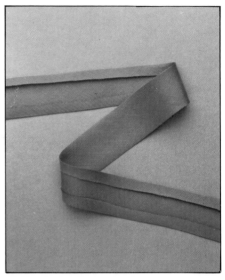

1 With wrong sides together, baste and stitch the seam. Trim the seam allowances to $\frac{1}{4}$in (6mm) and press together. Cut a bias strip of fabric the length required by $1\frac{3}{4}$in (4cm) wide.

2 Turn under $\frac{1}{4}$in (6mm) along both edges and press flat. This will make a finished binding of approximately $\frac{5}{8}$in (1.5cm).

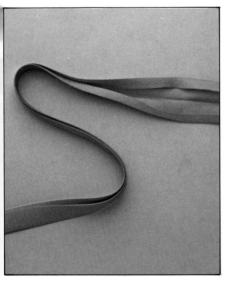

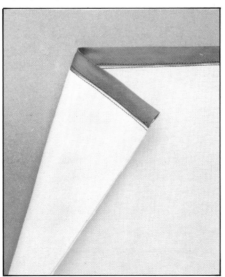

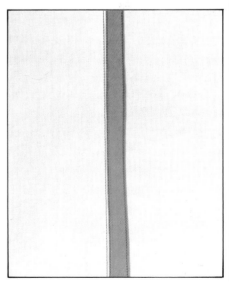

3 With the right side of the binding facing outward, fold the binding in half and press carefully so that the foldline can be seen clearly.

4 Place the binding over the seam allowance, enclosing all raw edges so that each half of the binding meets the stitching line of the seam (shown here for clarity). Pin, baste and stitch through all layers close to the edges. Press.

5 Press bound seam flat to one side, toward the back on underarm and shoulder seams, downward on yoke or armhole seams; pin, baste and stitch through all thicknesses close to foldline.

Simon Butcher

Easy binding

Here is a quick and easy method for binding raw edges. No hand sewing is necessary apart from initial basting. This method is ideal for open-weave fabrics, fabrics which ravel easily, or for bonded fabrics, on which hand sewing is difficult; on bonded fabrics, it is advisable to glue the binding in place before machine-stitching. Use large stitches.

The raw edges on any garment or article can be bound in a contrasting fabric or bias binding.

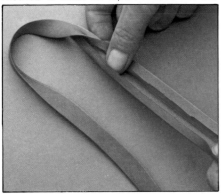

1 The width of the binding will depend on the finished width of the bound edge. If using fabric, cut a bias strip the length required and approximately 1¾in (4cm) wide for a ⅝in (1.5cm) finished bound edge. Turn in ¼in (6mm) along both edges and press flat.

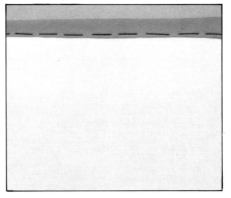

2 With right side of binding facing outward, fold binding in half over the raw edge. Pin and baste through all thicknesses. If using bonded fabrics, glue binding in place.

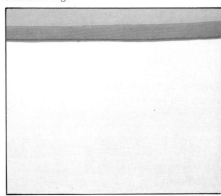

3 Stitch through all thicknesses close to the inner edge of the binding. Be sure the binding has been caught in the stitching on the reverse side. Remove basting and press.

Evening jacket and bag

This dazzling jacket is made in a mesh fabric with cleverly bound seams. The matching clutch bag has a decorative strip which echoes the lines of the seams on the jacket. Add tassels at the neck and to the bag for extra sparkle. The twosome will turn a simple dress into a stunning outfit.

Adapting the pattern

Measurements
The jacket is made by adapting the patterns for the basic jacket and the basic dress from the Stitch by Stitch Pattern Pack, available in sizes 10 to 20 (corresponding to sizes 8 to 18 in ready-made clothes). The evening bag measures 10×7in (25×18cm approx.).

Materials
3 sheets of tracing paper 36×40in (90×100cm approx.)
Flexible curve
Yardstick, right triangle

1 Trace the jacket back pattern, omitting the hem allowance and the back neck seam allowance. These edges are to be bound.

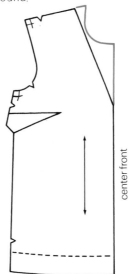

2 To make the jacket front pattern, trace the jacket front, omitting the hem allowance, front neck and center front seam allowance.
3 To draw the high, round neckline, lay the tracing of the front over the basic dress front pattern, aligning the shoulder line, center front line and side bust dart. Trace the dress neck cutting line from shoulder to center front and mark the remaining center front line.

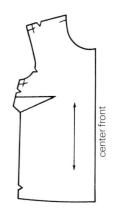

4 On the tracing, omit the neck seam allowance. The neck and front edges are bound.

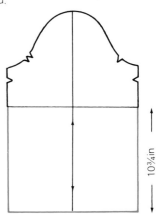

5 Trace the jacket sleeve pattern. Measuring from the lower edge of the

sleeve, extend the sleeve 10¾in (27.5cm) for a size 10, adding an extra ¼in (6mm) for each larger size. Extend the grain line to the top and bottom of the sleeve.

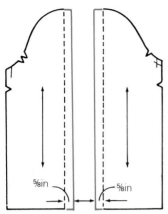

6 To separate the sleeve pattern into two parts, cut along the center grain line. Add a ⅝in (1.5cm) seam allowance to each of the cut edges. Mark the grain line on both sleeve pieces.

Bag

If using a woven fabric for the bag, you will need to make the decorative strip (see step 5) of coordinating ribbon or braid with firm edges.

For a crisp finish, the bag is stiffened with three pieces of medium-weight cardboard. If you prefer, the cardboard can be omitted and stiff canvas or heavy interfacing can be used instead. The lines of stitching which prevent the cardboard from moving are also the foldlines. The bag could also be quilted, but will need batting between the fabric and cardboard.

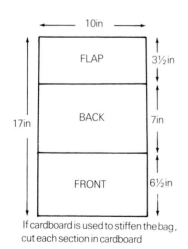

If cardboard is used to stiffen the bag, cut each section in cardboard

1 Draw a rectangle 10×17in (25× 43.5cm). This will be the main bag pattern before shaping. The rectangle is divided into three sections: front, back and flap. Measure up from lower edge of rectangle 6½in (16.5cm) and draw a line across at this point.
2 Measure up a further 7in (18cm) and

draw a line across. The remaining section, which will be the flap of the bag, is 3½in (9cm) deep. The lines drawn across the rectangle indicate the stitching lines.

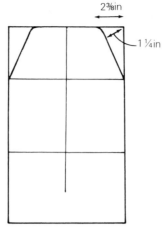

3 The flap is shaped at the top corners. Measure in from one top corner 2⅜in (6cm) and mark. Draw the corner curve from the top stitching line to this mark, to the required shape. As a guide, the center of the curve is 1¼in (3cm) in from the corner. Fold the rectangle in half lengthwise and trace the shape.

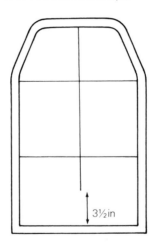

4 For the strip position, draw a line down the center of the rectangle to within 3½in (9cm) of the bottom edge. This will indicate the central positioning line for the strip. Add a ⅜in (1cm) seam allowance to all edges of the pattern.
5 To make the strip pattern, draw a rectangle 13¾×⅝in (35×1.5cm). This will be cut once in main fabric. If using fabric which ravels for the bag, use ribbon or braid for the strip.

Directions for making

Suggested fabrics
Jacket—mesh, net, crepe, chiffon, satin, velvet, velveteen.
Bag—bonded fabrics, soft leathers, velvet, satin, leather-like and suede fabrics.

Key to adjusted pattern pieces

A	Jacket front	Cut 2
B	Jacket back	Cut 1 on fold
C	Sleeve back	Cut 2
D	Sleeve front	Cut 2
E	Bag	Cut 1 each main, lining and inter-lining or card-board
F	Bag strip	Cut 1

Materials
Jacket
  36in (90cm)-wide fabric with or without nap:
    Sizes 10–14: 2¼yd (2m)
    Sizes 16–20: 2⅜yd (2.1m)
  36in (90cm)-wide fabric for bias binding for all sizes: 1⅛yd (1m)
  Hook and eye
Evening bag
  20×14in (50×35cm) main fabric
  20×12in (50×30cm) lining
  20×12in (50=30cm) interlining
  Two pieces stiff cardboard 6¾×10in (17×25cm)
  One piece stiff cardboard 3½×10in (9×25cm)
  ½yd (.4m) of ⅝in (1.5cm)-wide ribbon
  Button, 3 tassels (optional), thread

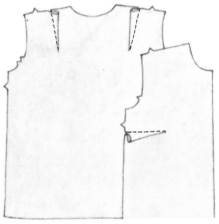

1 With right sides together, fold, baste and stitch the back shoulder darts and the front side bust darts. Press.

2 With wrong sides together, baste and stitch the shoulder and side seams. Trim the seam allowances to ¼in (6mm) and press together.

John Hutchinson

3 Cut a bias strip of fabric the length required to bind each seam and 1⅝in (4cm) wide. Bind the seam allowances together using the conspicuous bound seam method as shown on page 55.
4 Press the shoulder and side seams toward the jacket back and stitch down flat, stitching close to the outer edge of the binding as directed on page 55. Press.

5 Cut a bias strip of fabric 1¾in (4cm) wide, to bind the center front, neck and hem edges of the jacket. Join strips to

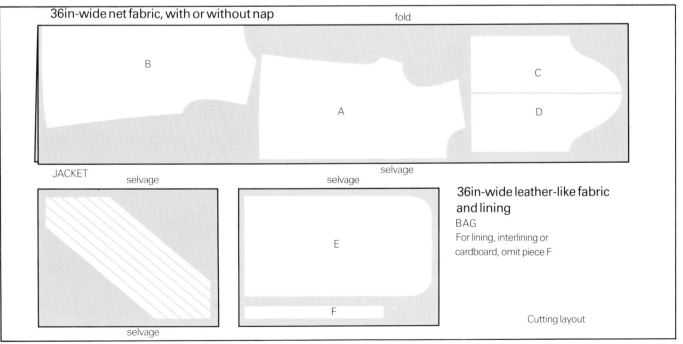

36in-wide net fabric, with or without nap

fold

B

C

A

D

selvage

JACKET

selvage

selvage

E

F

selvage

36in-wide leather-like fabric and lining
BAG
For lining, interlining or cardboard, omit piece F

Cutting layout

Brian Mayor

make up the length if necessary. Bind the edges using the easy binding method as shown on page 56. Miter the binding at the corners. The finished width of the binding will be approximately ⅝in (1.5cm).

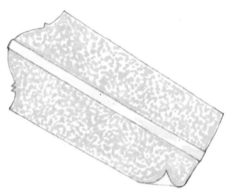

6 With wrong sides together, baste and stitch the two sleeve pieces together. Trim the seam allowance and bind following the bound seam method shown on page 55.
Press seam allowance toward back edge of sleeve and stitch flat. Press. Run two rows of gathering stitches around sleeve cap between notches.

7 With right sides together, baste and stitch the underarm seam of the sleeve. Press the seam allowances together and stitch the seam again ¼in (6mm) away from the first row of stitching, Zig-zag to finish raw edges, stitching close to second row of stitching. Trim the seam allowance to the zig-zag stitching. Press seam allowance toward the back edge of the sleeve.

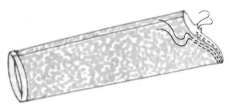

8 Cut a bias strip 1¾in (4cm) wide to fit the sleeve hem plus seam allowances. Join the strip to form a circle and bind the lower edge of the sleeve by the easy binding method as shown on page 56. Repeat for the other sleeve.

9 With wrong sides together, and notches and seams matching, pin the sleeve into the armhole and pull up the gathering threads to ease in the fullness. Baste, spreading the gathers evenly around the sleeve cap. Stitch the seam.

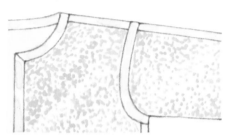

10 Trim the seam allowance to ¼in (6mm). Bind the seam allowances together, and stitch the bound seam down flat to the sleeve, using the conspicuous bound seam method. Repeat with other sleeve.
11 Sew a hook and eye on the inside of the front neck edge and finish with a decorative clasp or brooch. Attach tassels if desired.

Bag

Note: More design detail can be added to the bag with rows of topstitching, done before the lining is stitched in place. If using heavy woven stiffening, omit the cardboard and cut the interlining to the same shape as the main bag, omitting the ⅜in (1cm) seam allowances. Slip the interlining between the lining and main fabric. Machine-baste interlining over marked stitching lines, or proceed as for ordinary interfacing.

1 Make a loop for the bag fastening from thin cord or a narrow strip of the main fabric doubled and stitched along edge. The loop should be long enough to fit around the button plus ¾in (2cm) extra.

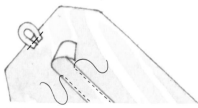

2 With the wrong side of the decorative strip to the right side of the outer bag section, stitch the strip in place along the positioning line on the pattern, centering it over the line. At the end of the strip near the flap, slip the button loop between the strip and the flap before stitching across end. Stitch through all thicknesses to secure loop.

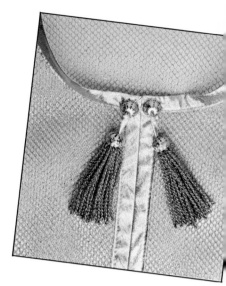

3 With right sides together, pin or tape the bag section and the lining section together, pinning within the seam allowance. Keeping the button loop folded back inside so that it is not caught in the seam allowance, stitch around the edges of the bag, leaving the lower edge open. Trim seams to ¼in (6mm) and clip curves.
4 Turn the bag right side out through opening. Cut smallest cardboard piece to shape of flap and slip between the two layers. Push cardboard to end. Stitch along first stitching line through all thicknesses, avoid cardboard.

5 Slip the second piece of cardboard between the two layers and stitch along the second stitching line as before. Insert the third piece of cardboard. Turn in the seam allowance at the open end and stitch to close, stitching close to the edge through all thicknesses but avoiding the cardboard.
6 Fold the bag into shape along the stitching lines. The sides may be joined by hand, using overcasting or backstitch, or by machine. If using a machine, work close to the edges and be sure to fasten the ends securely. To complete the bag, sew a button to the front at the end of the decorative strip. A gold tassel can add sparkle.

Sewing/COURSE 69

*Making a seam roll
*Herringbone stitched hem
*Working with wool fabric
*Pattern for culottes: adapting the pattern: directions for making

Making a seam roll

A seam roll is a padded rolled shape that can be used when pressing seams. It will prevent marks from forming on the right side of the fabric. Its cylindrical shape makes it useful for pressing seams in awkward-to-get-at places such as sleeves and pants legs, especially on children's clothes. It can be made of a tube of cotton fabric stuffed with shredded foam rubber, or polyester fiberfill. Ideally, it should have one or more removable covers in fabrics appropriate for the fabric being pressed, such as a wool cover for wool fabric, cotton for cotton, etc. An emergency seam roll can be made with a rolled-up magazine covered with a sock or two (which must be colorfast). The following method is for making a permanent seam roll 10in (25cm) long.

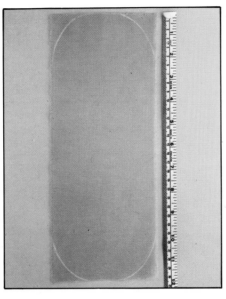

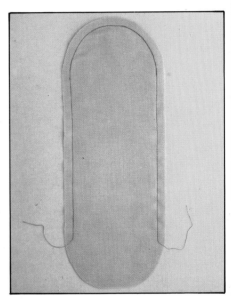

1 Cut two rectangles of cotton fabric 12 × 5in (30 × 12cm). Round off corners.

2 With right sides together, stitch the two pieces together taking a $\frac{3}{8}$in (1cm) seam allowance and leaving one end open.

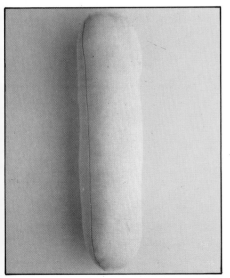

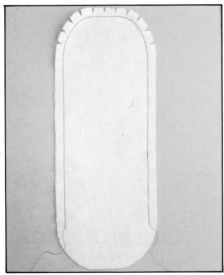

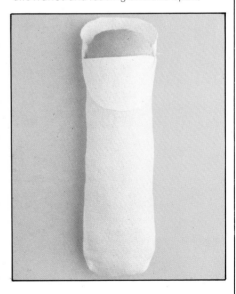

3 Turn the roll right side out and stuff carefully until a neat padded shape is formed. When roll is sufficiently padded, turn in the raw ends and slip stitch them together to close the end. The roll should be firm, but not too hard, to hold its shape in use.

4 For cover, cut two fabric rectangles from lightweight fabric 12 × 5in (30 × 12cm) and round off corners. Stitch around edge with right sides together, leaving one end open as before. Press carefully and clip curves along seam allowance.

5 Turn cover right side out, slide it over the padded roll and slip stitch to close. The cover can be removed for laundering or cleaning.

Simon Butcher

61

Herringbone stitched hem

Suitable hem finishes for woolen garments are bound hems, blindstitched hems, and herringbone stitched hems. The last is especially suitable for loosely woven woolens or for bulkier fabrics where the hem would be too thick with the raw edge turned under twice, as on the culottes shown opposite. Start by marking the hemline with a row of basting stitches.

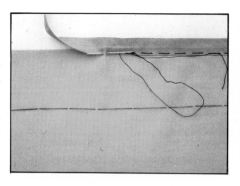

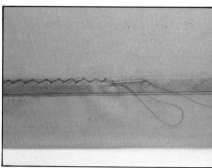

1 With the right side of the hem allowance uppermost, baste and stitch the binding close to the raw edge. The machine-stitching should be close to the edge of the binding.

2 Trim away any extra hem allowance so that none extends above the binding and, using herringbone stitch, sew the free edge of the binding to the skirt, taking care not to pull the stitches tightly.

Working with wool fabric

When working with woolen fabric you should take a little extra care in preparing and handling it to ensure a successful garment. It may be difficult to find the right side of woolen fabrics, as each side often looks the same. The weave of many woolens helps to identify the right side as will the selvage, which is smoother on the right side than on the wrong side. Some woolen fabric is partly preshrunk, but it is best to shrink the fabric before cutting out, even if it is to be dry cleaned. This can be done by holding the fabric lengthwise on the grain and placing it between the folds of a wet sheet or large piece of clean white fabric for ten or twelve hours. Remove it from the sheet and lay out flat to dry completely. When it is dry, press on the wrong side with iron and press cloth.

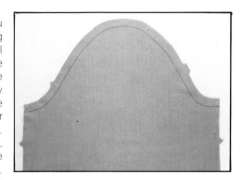

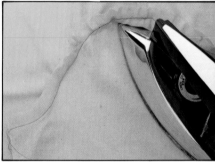

1 Lay out the pattern pieces as directed and use sharp scissors to cut out. Cut one thickness at a time if necessary. To prevent the fabric from stretching, stay-stitch any curved edges.

2 Wool can be shrunk easily, which is an advantage when removing excess fullness. To shrink out the fullness in a sleeve cap so that the cap is the exact size and shape of the armhole, press the sleeve and armhole seams together from the sleeve side after seaming.

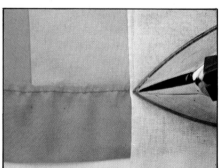

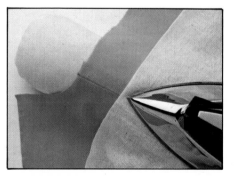

3 To shrink the fullness out of a hem, run a row of gathering stitches $\frac{1}{4}$in (5mm) from the raw edge. Pull up the thread until this edge lies flat. Place a cloth or piece of brown paper between the fabric and hem and press gently with the tip of the iron and a damp cloth. This will shrink out the fullness. Leave to dry and then complete the hem.

4 To prevent the imprint of a hem, dart or seam allowance from appearing on the right side of the garment, slip a piece of cloth or paper between the garment and the edge. Cut darts and press open to eliminate bulk. To prevent ridges from forming along the seamline when pressing from the right side, use a seam roll.

5 When pressing from the right side of the fabric, protect the wool by placing a layer of clean white woolen fabric between the garment and the press cloth.

Culottes

Pleats at the waistline add a fashionable touch to these culottes, made in firmly woven wool.

Adapting the pattern

Measurements: The culottes are adapted from the basic pants pattern in the Stitch by Stitch Pattern Pack, available in sizes 10 to 20, corresponding to sizes 8 to 18 in ready-made clothes.

Materials
2 sheets of tracing paper 36×40in (90×100cm approx.)
Flexible curve, yardstick

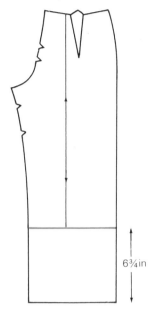

6¾in

1 Trace the basic pants pattern. To mark the length, measure up 6¾in (17cm) from the hem edge of the pattern and mark in the new cutting line. This measurement includes a 2½in (6.5cm) hem allowance. Extend the grain line to the top and bottom edge of the pattern.

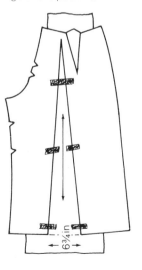

6¾in

2 Cut along this line from the lower edge to the waist seamline only. Lay the pattern over paper and open out the lower edge by 6¾in (17cm). Tape in place. Re-draw the hemline at this point and mark the grain line through the center of the insertion as shown.

John Hutchinson

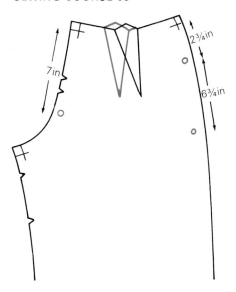

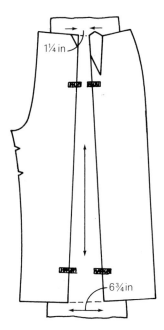

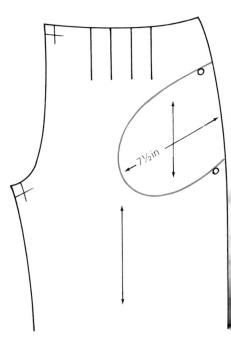

3 Re-draw the waist dart by moving the dart point so that it is centered between the center back and the side seams.
To mark the pocket position at the side seam, measure down the side seamline from the waist seamline 2¾in (7cm) and a further 6¾in (17cm) to represent the top and bottom of the pocket.

4 To mark the bottom of the zipper position, measure down the center back seamline from the waist seamline 7in (18cm) and draw a circle.

6 Cut along this line to separate the pattern. Lay the two halves of the pattern over paper. Spread the pattern 1¼in (3cm) at waist seamline and 6¾in (17cm) at lower edge. Tape the pattern pieces in place. Re-draw the hem and waistline. Mark the grain line through the center of the insertion.

9 To make the pocket pattern, draw shape of pocket between two marks on front as shown, using a flexible curve. The pocket should be 7½in (19cm) deep and should slant down.

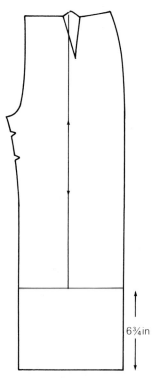

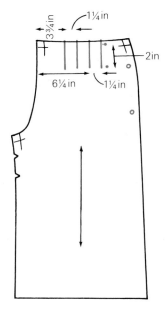

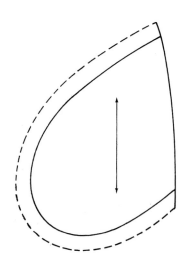

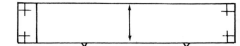

5 Trace the basic pants front pattern. To mark the length, measure up from the lower edge of the pants 6¾in (17cm) and draw the new cutting line. This measurement includes a 2½in (6.5cm) hem allowance. Extend the grain line to the top and bottom edges of the pattern as for the back.

7 To mark the tuck positions at the waistline, measure in along the waist seamline from the center front cutting line 3¾in (9.5cm) and a further 1¼in (3cm) and mark. The 1¼in (3cm) allowance is the width of the first tuck.

8 For the second tuck, measure in from center front cutting line 6¼in (16cm) and a further 1¼in (3cm). The 1¼in (3cm) allowance is width of second tuck. Draw tuck lines parallel to straight grain making them 2in (5cm) long from waist seamline. For the pocket position mark the side seam as for the back.

10 Trace the pocket shape from the front. Mark the grain line for the pocket parallel to the grain line of the front. Trace the pocket shape and mark the grain line. Add ⅝in (1.5cm) seam allowance all around the curved edge. (Here the cutting line is shown as a broken line and the seamline is solid.)

11 To make the waistband pattern, use the basic pants waistband but reposition the notches at the side seams because the culottes have a center back opening. The underlap is shown at the left-hand end.

Cutting layout for culottes
54in-wide fabric with or without nap

fold

selvages

Key to adjusted pattern pieces
A	Front	Cut 2
B	Back	Cut 2
C	Waistband	Cut 1

D Pocket   Cut 4

Interfacing: use piece C cut to half width only

Directions for making

Suggested fabrics
Double knits, jersey, sailcloth, wool, linen, velour, pinwale corduroy.

Materials
54in (140cm)-wide fabric with or without nap:
  Sizes 10–14: $2\frac{1}{4}$yd (2m)
  Sizes 16–20: $2\frac{3}{8}$yd (2.1m)
36in (90cm)-wide interfacing: for all sizes: $\frac{1}{4}$yd (.2m)
7in (18cm) zipper
Matching thread
Pants hook and eye

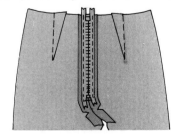

1 Working from the wrong side of the fabric, fold, pin and baste the front tucks in position at each side of the center front. The fold of each tuck should be pressed away from the center front on the right side. Each tuck takes $1\frac{1}{4}$in (3cm) fabric allowance. With right sides together, pin, baste and stitch center front seam to within $\frac{5}{8}$in (1.5cm) of crotch.

2 Working from the wrong side of the garment on the back sections, pin, baste

and stitch the darts. With right sides together, pin, baste and stitch the center back seam from the marked point at the zipper position to within $\frac{5}{8}$in (1.5cm) of crotch. Press seam open and clip curves.

3 Working from right side, position zipper under zipper opening. Pin, baste and stitch zipper in place. Press gently from the right side.

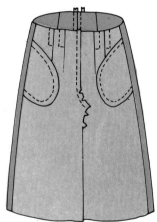

4 Make and attach the pockets as directed in Volume 5, page 72, matching pockets to pocket positions on front and back. With right sides together, pin, baste and stitch the side seams from waist to hem. Press the seams open.

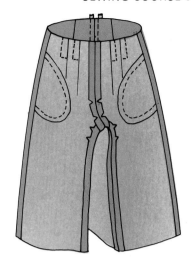

5 With right sides together, pin, baste and stitch inner leg seams, clip curves and press open. Complete crotch seam and press open.

6 Following directions from basic pants pattern, make and attach waistband, noting that the opening is at the center back. Attach the pants hook to the overlap on the waistband, and the eye to the underlap.

7 Turn up the hem allowance on each leg and complete, using the method shown on page 62. Decorative topstitching can be worked on the waistband and hem edges if desired.

Terri Lawlor

*Pocket with welt
*Decorative snaps
*Pattern for a double-breasted blouse:
adapting the pattern;
directions for making

Pocket with welt

A pocket made with a welt is strong as well as decorative because the flap or welt protects the pocket opening from wear and tear. Such pockets are often found on tailored garments, such as suits or coats, but can look just as attractive on a more delicate fabric or lighter garment, such as the blouse on page 68. The welt pocket is made by cutting an opening in the garment and finishing the construction in a similar way to a bound buttonhole—the difference is that the pocket has an extension covering the opening which is known as the welt or welt flap.

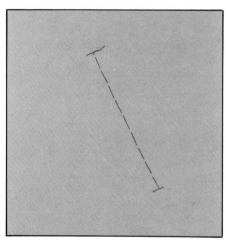

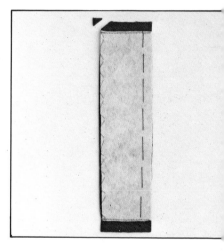

1 Mark the position of the pocket with a row of basting stitches. A stitch across each end will mark the length of the pocket. If making more than one pocket— for example, on each side of the front of a garment—be sure to make the pocket lines the same length.

2 Baste the interfacing to one half of the pocket welt on the wrong side and catch-stitch the interfacing to the foldline Fold the welt in half, right sides together. Baste and stitch across the ends. Trim the interfacing close to the stitching. Trim the other seam allowances and cut across the corners.

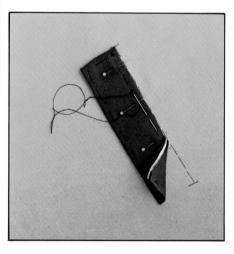

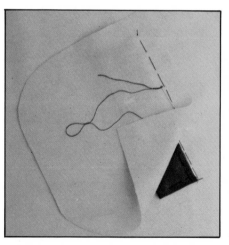

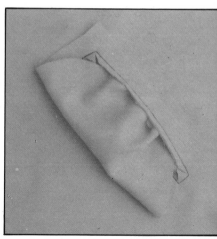

3 Turn the welt right side out and baste around stitched edges. Press flat. Pin the welt to the right side of the garment with the folded edge downward and the raw edges along the basting line. Baste $\frac{1}{4}$in (5mm) in from the raw edges.

4 With right sides together, pin one pocket section to the garment over the welt. Place the seamline of the pocket $\frac{1}{4}$in (5mm) above the center basting line for the pocket position. Baste in place.

5 Turn the garment to the wrong side and stitch around the pocket position, stitching $\frac{1}{4}$in (5mm) from either side of the center marking and across each end. Cut through the garment and pocket piece between the stitching and clip diagonally into corners. Pull pocket piece gently through opening to wrong side and baste around opening.

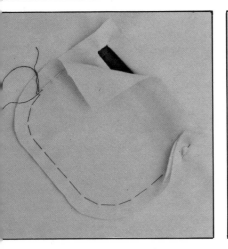

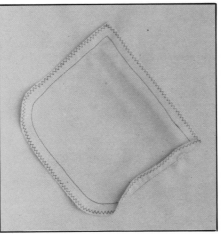

6 Press the welt piece upward over the opening. On the wrong side, with right sides together, baste the second pocket piece over the first. Trim one pocket piece to fit the other if necessary.

7 Stitch the pocket pieces together beginning at one upper corner and around all edges, stitching across the triangle formed by clipping at the corners, then around the pocket bag and across the triangle at the other end. Finally, stitch across the top edges through three thicknesses, following the previous stitching line. Remove all basting and press. Finish the outer edges of the pocket bag with zig-zag stitch.

8 On the right side, slip stitch the side edges of the welt to the garment with small, invisible stitches. Alternatively, the welt can be topstitched close to these edges to hold it in place. Press.

Decorative snaps

A decorative snap is a type of fastener consisting of a decorative pronged section which locks into the socket part of the fastener and a pronged ring which locks into the stud section; it is both pretty and practical.

They are used to fasten the double-breasted blouse on page 68, but they could also be used on other kinds of garment. Heavy-duty snaps are useful on pants, jackets, jeans, vests and skirts in heavier fabrics such as denim and gabardine. Lightweight snaps are often used on babies' terrycloth garments but would be just as practical on adults' clothes such as lingerie, sportswear and lightweight casual clothing.

It is advisable to practice applying the snaps on a spare piece of fabric, as they can easily be torn out if not applied correctly. If the fabric to be used is very thin, apply the snaps to double or triple thickness (for example, to interfaced and faced areas), or reinforce the wrong side with tape or fabric before applying the snaps. If special pliers are needed, they are usually sold with the snaps.

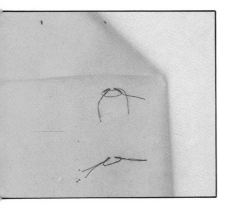

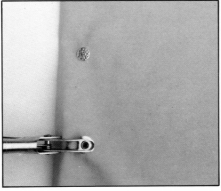

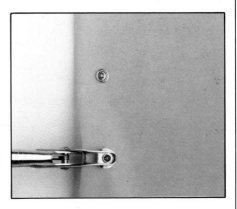

1 Mark the positions of the snaps with tailor's tacks so that they are clearly visible from both sides.

2 Place the decorative pronged section of the snap in the top jaw of the pliers (with the solid area). Place socket section of snap with raised side upward on lower jaw of pliers (with the hole). Slide fabric between pliers and position carefully over the mark on the right side of the garment fabric. Squeeze firmly until snap is secure.

3 Remove and turn over the rubber ring in the top jaw. Insert the plain pronged section of the snap. Place stud section of snap with the ball side down into the lower jaw of pliers. Place top jaw to fastener position on wrong or underside of garment and squeeze firmly when in place.

Double-breasted blouse

A double-breasted blouse is a stylish variation on a classic look. It can be made in a wide variety of fabrics and looks good with pants or a sleek skirt. Decorative snaps emphasize the style.

Adapting the pattern
The blouse pattern is adapted from the basic shirt from the Stitch by Stitch Pattern Pack, available in sizes 10 to 20.

Materials
3 sheets of tracing paper 36×40in (90×100cm approx.)
Flexible curve, yardstick
Right triangle

1 Pin the front yoke to the shirt front and the back yoke to the shirt back, overlapping the ⅝in (1.5cm) seam allowance so seamlines are aligned. Trace both complete pieces leaving extra paper at center front edge.

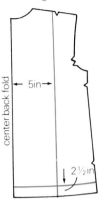

2 To make the back pattern, shorten the length of the basic back pattern by 2½in (6cm). Draw a line 5in (13cm) in from and parallel to the center back from the shoulder to the lower edge.

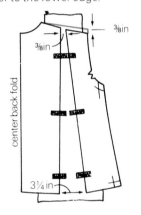

3 Cut along this line and spread the pattern by ⅜in (1cm) at shoulder seamline and 3¼in (8cm) at lower edge. Insert and tape paper behind the slash. Raise shoulder cutting line ⅜in (1cm) at armhole edge and draw the new shoulder line tapering into the cutting line at the neck edge.

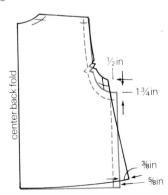

4 Adjust the side seam cutting line, by adding ½in (1.3cm) to side edge at armhole curve and measuring ⅜in (1cm) in from the side cutting line at the lower

edge. Draw the new side cutting line from the armhole to the lower edge, dropping lower edge by ⅝in (1.5cm). Mark in the seam allowance and taper new hem cutting line into the raised line at the lower edge.

5 To lower the armhole at the side seam measure down the new side seam from the armhole seamline 1¾in (4.5cm) and, using the flexible curve, redraw the armhole seamline from the shoulder to the side seam. Add the ⅝in (1.5cm) seam allowance to the armhole edge.

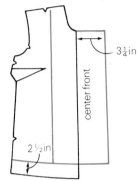

6 To make the front pattern, first trace the adjusted front pattern.
Shorten length of front pattern by 2½in (6cm). Add 3¼in (8cm) to front edge and mark in the ⅝in (1.5cm) seamline. To remove the bust dart and enlarge the pattern, draw a line from the dart point up to the shoulder line and down to lower edge keeping it parallel to the center front.

7 Cut along this line as far as dart point from both sides. Do not cut completely through pattern. Close dart and tape in place. Lay pattern over the paper ready to tape down. Spread pattern ⅜in (1cm) at shoulder seam and 6in (15.5cm) at lower edge. Tape in place.

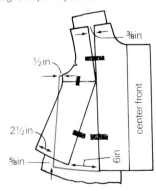

8 To redraw the side seam cutting line, add ½in (1.3cm) to side edge at armhole curve, and at the lower edge measure in 2½in (6.5cm) from cutting line and mark. Draw the new cutting line from the armhole to the lower edge, extending it by ⅝in (1.5cm). Taper line into cutting line at the lower edge.

9 Raise the shoulder cutting line by ⅜in (1cm) at armhole edge. Draw the shoulder line, tapering into the original cutting line

at the neck edge. Lower the armhole by measuring down the new side seamline 1¾in (4.5cm) from original seamline and, using a flexible curve, redraw the armhole seamline from the shoulder to the side seam. Add ⅝in (1.5cm) seam allowance to armhole edge. Mark the grain line parallel to the center front.

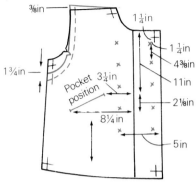

10 For the pocket position, measure down center front from the neck cutting line 11in (28cm) and a further 2⅛in (5.5cm). Mark each point. Using a right triangle, measure in 3¼in (8.5cm) from first point and 8¼in (21cm) from the second. Draw a line to connect these two points as shown. This will indicate the pocket line.
11 For the snap positions, mark the top position 1¼in (3cm) down and in from the neck edge and front edge. Mark the other four at 4⅜in (11cm) intervals. Mark the corresponding five fastening positions 5in (13cm) in from front edge.

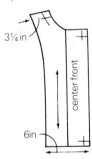

12 To make the front and back neck facing patterns, lay tracing paper over the new front pattern and trace the front neck and the shoulder cutting line to a depth of 3¼in (8.5cm). Trace the hem edge from the front for 6in (15cm). Draw the outer edge of the facing from the shoulder to the lower edge as shown. Mark the seamlines and the grain line, parallel to the front edge.

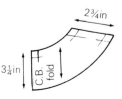

13 To make the back neck facing pattern, trace the back neck and shoulder cutting

John Hutchinson

line to a depth of 2¾in (7cm) and along center back line to a depth of 3¼in (8cm). Using a flexible curve, connect these two points for the outer curved edge of the facing. Mark the grain line and indicate that center back is on a fold.

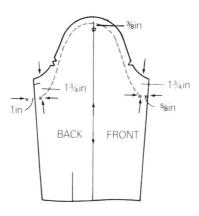

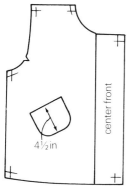

14 To make the pocket pattern, draw the shape of the pocket between the pocket positions on the blouse front as shown. The pocket should be 4½in (11.5cm) deep with rounded lower corners.

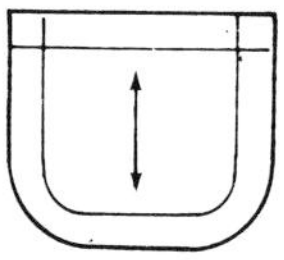

15 Trace the pocket shape and mark in the grain line parallel to the side edges. Add ⅝in (1.5cm) seam allowance to all edges.

16 To make the pocket welt pattern, draw a rectangle 6½ × 3in (16.5 × 7.5cm). A ⅝in (1.5cm) seam allowance has been included in these measurements. Mark foldline along the center of rectangle and grain line parallel to side edges.

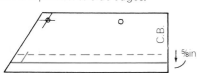

17 To make the collar pattern, trace the pointed collar pattern from the Pattern Pack. Make the collar ⅝in (1.5cm) narrower as shown. The finished width will be 2in (5cm). Mark seamlines and indicate that center back is on a fold.
18 To make the sleeve pattern, trace the shirt sleeve pattern, raising the seamline at center of sleeve cap by ⅜in (1cm). To reshape the armhole, measure down the back underarm seamline from seamline of underarm curve 1¾in (4.5cm), and out by 1in (2.5cm). Mark.
19 Measure down the front underarm seamline from seamline of underarm curve 1¾in (4.5cm) and out by ⅝in

(1.5cm). Mark. Using a flexible curve, redraw new sleeve cap seamline.
20 Add ⅝in (1.5cm) seam allowance to sleeve cap. To ensure that the sleeve measurements are correct, measure around the sleeve cap seamline from the center to the back underarm seam and to the front underarm seam. Measure the blouse back and front armholes along the seamlines. The measurement of the sleeve cap should be ⅝in (1.5cm) larger than armhole at both back and front for ease.

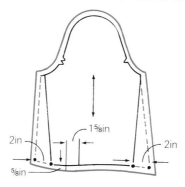

21 At the lower edge of the sleeve, measure out from the underarm cutting line 2in (5cm) on each side and redraw both underarm seamlines from the lower edge to the underarm curve. Add ⅝in (1.5cm) seam allowance to both edges. At lower edge add ⅝in (1.5cm) to length of sleeve. Re-mark the sleeve opening by moving it out 1⅝in (4cm).

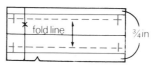

22 To make the cuff pattern, trace the basic shirt cuff. Mark the fold line, seam allowance and grain line. Mark the position for the snap in the center of one half of the finished width of cuff as shown above.

Directions for making

Suggested fabrics
Poplin, crepe, shantung, velveteen, pique, denim, gabardine.

John Hutchinson

Materials
36in (90cm)-wide fabric with or without nap:
Sizes 10-12: 2⅞yd (2.6m)
Size 14, 16: 3½yd (3.1m)
Size 18, 20: 3⅝yd (3.3m)
45in (115cm)-wide fabric with or without nap:
Sizes 10-16: 2⅝yd (2.4m)
Sizes 18, 20: 2¾yd (2.5m)
36in (90cm)-wide interfacing:
For all sizes: 1⅛yd (1m)
Shoulder pads
Matching thread, 12 snaps

Key to adjusted pattern pieces

A	Back	Cut 1 on fold
B	Front	Cut 2
C	Front and neck facing	Cut 2
D	Sleeve	Cut 2
E	Back neck facing	Cut 1 on fold
F	Pocket	Cut 4
G	Pocket welt	Cut 2
H	Collar	Cut 2 on fold
I	Cuff	Cut 2

Interfacing: use pieces **C** Cut 2, **E** Cut 1 on fold, **G** Cut 2 to half width only, **H** Cut 1 on fold, **I** Cut 2 to half width only.

1 Baste the wrong side of the interfacing to the wrong side of the blouse front and back neck edges. Mark the position of the pockets on both front pieces and make a welt pocket at both positions as shown on page 66. With right sides together, baste and stitch the shoulder seams. Finish seam allowance and press open.

2 Baste the wrong side of the interfacing to the wrong side of one collar section. With right sides together, baste and stitch the two collar pieces together, leaving the neck edge open. Trim the interfacing close to the stitching. Trim the other seam allowances and clip across the corners.

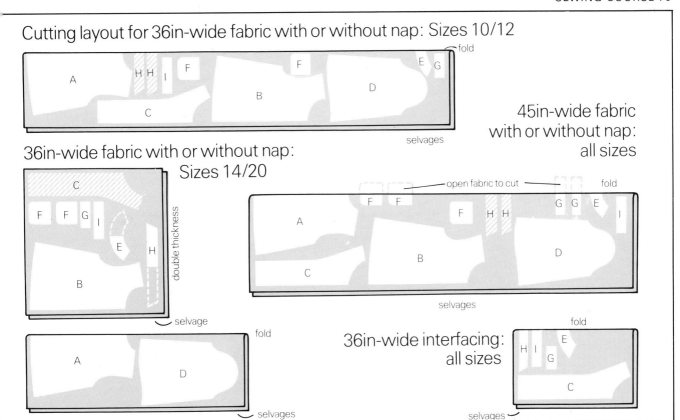

Cutting layout for 36in-wide fabric with or without nap: Sizes 10/12

45in-wide fabric with or without nap: all sizes

36in-wide fabric with or without nap: Sizes 14/20

36in-wide interfacing: all sizes

3 Turn the collar right side out and baste around outer edges; press. With the interfaced edge of the collar next to the garment, baste the collar flat to the neck edge.

4 With right sides together, baste and stitch the front and back neck facings together at the shoulder seams. Press seams open and finish the outer edges of the facings together.

5 With right sides together and shoulder seams matching; baste and stitch facings to neck edge and front edges over collar. Grade seam allowances, trimming interfacing close to stitching. Clip seam allowances and across corners.

6 Turn the facings to the inside and baste around the stitched edges. Press. Catch-stitch the facings to the shoulder seams. With right sides together, baste and stitch the side seams. Finish and press seams open.

7 Make the continuous lap sleeve opening at the lower edge of the sleeves as directed for the shirt sleeves in Volume 5, page 63. Stitch the sleeve seams and press open. Run two rows of gathering stitches around the sleeve cap and the lower edge.

8 Make the cuff as directed for the skirt pattern. Volume 5, page 64. Gather the lower edge of the sleeve to fit the cuff and attach the cuff to the sleeve as directed for the shirt, in Volume 5, page 64. Omit the buttonhole.

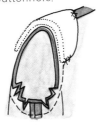

9 With right sides together and notches, seams and shoulder points matching; pin,

baste and stitch the sleeve into the armhole, easing in the fullness around the sleeve cap to fit. Clip the underarm curve and finish the seams together. Sew the shoulder pads to the inside as shown in Volume 9, page 61.

10 At the lower edge of the blouse turn up the hem, taking a ¾in (2cm) hem allowance and machine stitch. Attach the snaps to the blouse fronts and cuffs in the positions indicated on the pattern, following the directions on page 67. If you do not want to use decorative snaps, make buttonholes down the right and sew buttons at the marked points on right and left fronts. Alternatively, attach ordinary snaps in these positions and sew small decorative buttons on top of each to cover them.

*Making an arrowhead tack
*Topstitched knife pleats
*Understitched knife pleats
*Pattern for a pleated dress:
 adapting the pattern;
 directions for making

Making an arrowhead tack

The arrowhead tack provides a decorative and secure finish to the ends of pleats, darts and pockets. It is a good method to use when repairing a pleat that has split at the end of the stitching. Use buttonhole twist or embroidery thread, such as pearl cotton, to make the tack.

If the arrowhead tack is purely decorative, it does not matter in which direction the point faces; if it is to be used for reinforcing a pleat or dart, the base of the arrowhead needs to be placed at the end of the dart with the point facing toward the dart, or at the beginning of a pleat with the point facing away from the pleat. This reinforces the dart or pleat so that it cannot tear open in wear.

1 Mark the triangular shape of the arrowhead tack with chalk or thread, making sure the arrow is centered over the fold of the pleat or dart. Work the tack with the point upward.

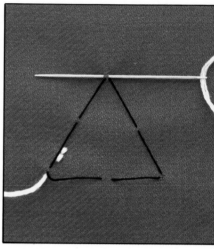

2 Starting at the lower left-hand corner, make two small stitches. Bring the needle out at the lower left-hand corner before beginning the arrowhead stitching. Take the needle to the point of the arrow and make a tiny stitch from right to left.

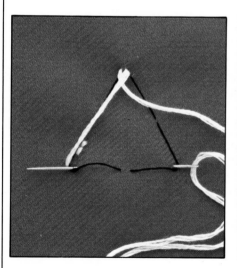

3 Bring the needle down to the lower right-hand corner. Insert and bring it out again at the lower left-hand corner.

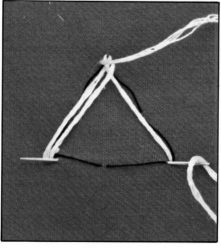

4 Take the needle back to the top and insert it from right to left as before but just below the previous stitch. Take the needle down and insert it just inside the first stitch on the right-hand corner, bringing it out just inside the thread on the left-hand side.

5 Repeat these steps, making the stitch at the point of the arrow slightly wider each time and placing the threads side by side until the triangle is completely filled in. Fasten the thread securely on the wrong side. The top of the arrow should have a herringbone formation of threads when finished.

Topstitched knife pleats

A knife pleat can be stitched in a variety of ways, but a topstitched knife pleat is the strongest because the pleat is stitched through three thicknesses. It is also a decorative method since the stitching shows on the right side of the garment and emphasizes the line of the pleats.

Topstitched knife pleats can be used on dresses, coats, blouses and skirts, and for extra effect, the topstitching can be of contrasting thread or a heavy-weight thread such as buttonhole twist. The length of the stitch and the distance between the pleat foldline and the top-stitching can be adjusted according to the fabric and garment style. A long stitch $\frac{3}{8}$in (1cm) from the foldline could be used on a thick wool coat, a short stitch $\frac{1}{8}$in (3mm) from the foldline might be used on a voile blouse. Usually, a medium stitch is used for topstitching, $\frac{1}{4}$in (5mm) from the pleat fold.

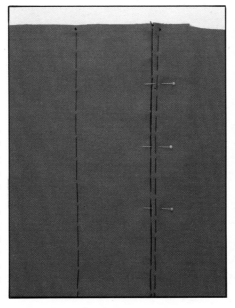

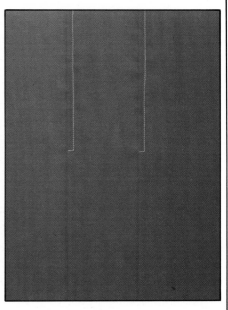

1 Transfer the pleat markings from the pattern to the garment with basting. Working from the right side, fold the first pleat into place, matching the pleat lines. Pin along the fold through all thicknesses. Baste the pleats through all thicknesses and press the folds, using a press cloth and removing pins first.

2 Topstitch the pleats in place, working from the right side and stitching $\frac{1}{4}$in (5mm) in from the fold of the pleat. Begin the stitching at the top of the pleat and at the end of the row of stitching continue stitching across the pleat to the fold. Bring the threads through to the wrong side and secure them. Remove basting and press.

Understitched knife pleats

Understitching a pleat gives the shape needed over a particular area, as on the hip or waistline of a skirt, without being conspicuous from the right side. The pleat is strong at the base and should not tear out even at the point of stress, because the stitching is continued through to the inner fold of the pleat.

Occasionally this method is used on shaped pleats where the top of the pleat is given a dart shaping, perhaps to take out excess fabric at waistline or yoke. This eliminates the need for further dart shaping and is worked in the same way as straight understitching except that the initial basted lines are shaped according to the pattern lines.

If an understitched pleat is too bulky, the excess fabric can be trimmed to within $\frac{3}{8}$in (1cm) of the stitching. The raw ends are then overcast together; however, the base of the pleat will drop slightly as the garment is worn.

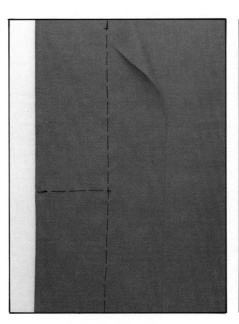

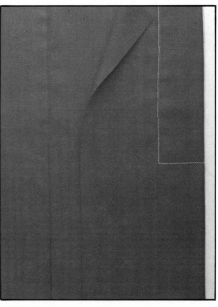

1 Mark the pleat foldlines. Fold each pleat into place. Pin and baste on the wrong side of the pleats along the pleat foldlines and across the pleat to the outer fold as shown.

2 On the wrong side, stitch from the top of the pleat close to the basting, down the length of the pleat and across to the outer fold. Secure the threads. Remove the basting and press, using a press cloth.

Simon Butcher

Peter Waldman

Pleated dress

The demure collar and cuffs on this attractive dress are made in a contrasting fabric. Details like these, plus the arrowhead tacks used to finish the pleats, give a designer look to a simple garment which would also be stylish in a solid color with plaid or contrasting trims.

Adapting the pattern

Measurements
The dress is made by adapting the pattern for the tie-neck blouse and basic skirt from the Stitch by Stitch Pattern Pack, available in sizes 10 to 20, corresponding to sizes 8 to 18 in ready-made clothes.

Materials
4 sheets of tracing paper 60×36in (150×90cm)
Flexible curve
Yardstick

Bodice and collar

1 To make the back pattern, trace basic blouse back, leaving extra paper at center back edge. Shorten pattern by 6½in (16.5cm) for size 10, adding an extra ¼in (5mm) to this amount for each larger size.

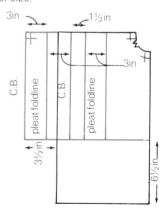

2 Add 3½in (9cm) to center back edge for the pleat allowance. This measurement includes a ⅝in (1.5cm) seam allowance at the center back seam.
3 To mark the pleat position lines, measure off 3, 6, 7½, 10½in (7.5, 15, 19, 26.5cm) from new center back cutting line and mark a series of parallel lines at these points. The first and third lines will be the pleat foldlines. The second and fourth lines will be the pleat position lines, (bring foldlines to these points when making pleats).

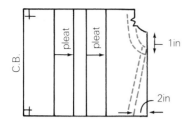

To lower the armhole, measure down from armhole seam 1in (2.5cm) and, using a flexible curve, redraw the armhole seamline at the notches. Mark the new armhole cutting line around the armhole ⅝in (1.5cm) from seamline.
To shape the side seam at the waist edge, measure in 2in (5cm) from cutting line and redraw the cutting line up to the armhole edge. Mark the seamline.

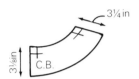

To make the back neck facing pattern, trace the back neck edge of the back yoke pattern and along the center back cutting line to a depth of 3⅛in (8cm). Trace the shoulder cutting line to 3¼in (8.5cm). Using a flexible curve, connect these two points to make the outer edge of the facing. Mark the seam allowance and the grain line parallel to the center back.

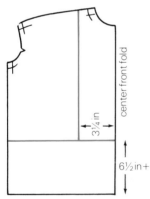

For the front, trace the blouse front pattern and shorten as for the back. For pleat allowance draw a parallel line ¼in (8.5cm) from center front.

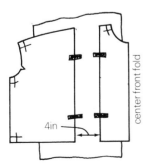

Cut along this line to separate the

pattern and spread by 4in (10cm). Insert and tape paper behind the slash.

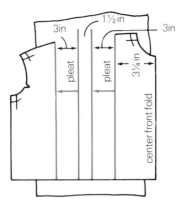

9 For the pleat position lines, measure 3¼, 6¼, 7¾, 10¾in (8.5, 16, 20, 27.5cm) from center front line and mark in a series of parallel lines at these points. The first and third lines are the foldlines and the second and fourth lines are the pleat position lines.

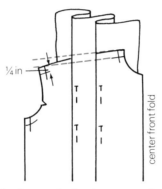

10 The front yoke line is at an angle to the top of the pleats, so they must be shaped: fold and pin the pleats into position, raise the yoke line by ¼in (5mm) at the armhole edge and, using a ruler, draw the new yoke line from the armhole, tapering into the original line at the neck edge. Mark the new cutting line ⅝in (1.5cm) from this line. Cut along the new cutting line and open out to see the shaping.

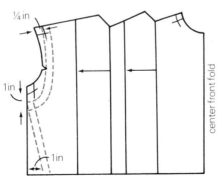

11 To shape the side seam at the waist edge, measure in 1in (2.5cm) from cutting line and redraw the cutting line up to the armhole edge. Mark the seamline and lower the armhole by 1in (2.5cm) as for the back. Move the armhole

cutting line in by ¼in (5mm) at the yoke edge before drawing new armhole cutting line. Mark seamline.

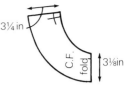

12 To make the front neck facing pattern, fold and pin the pleats into position on the blouse front pattern. Pin the yoke to the blouse front, matching the seamlines. Trace the neck edge, the center front to a depth of 3⅛in (8cm), and along the shoulder cutting line 3⅛in (8.5cm). Using a flexible curve, connect these two points for the outer edge of the facing. Mark seam allowances and the center front on the fold. The grain line is parallel to the center front.

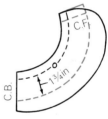

13 To make the collar pattern, trace the Peter Pan collar from the Pattern Pack and straighten the angle at the front edge as shown. Mark the seamline around the neck edge and from this line measure around the collar at intervals to a depth of 1¾in (4.5cm).

14 Using a flexible curve, redraw the new outer curved edge of the collar. Add ⅝in (1.5cm) seam allowance to outer edge and center back edge.

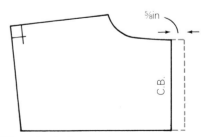

15 To make the back yoke pattern, trace the yoke back from the basic blouse. Add ⅝in (1.5cm) seam allowance to center back edge. Use the yoke front pattern from the basic blouse for the front yoke. Mark seamlines on each piece and trace grain lines.

Sleeve and cuff

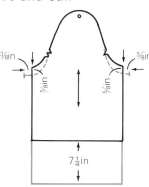

1 To make the sleeve pattern, trace the basic sleeve pattern, leaving extra paper at the lower edge. Add $7\frac{1}{4}$in (18.5cm) to the lower edge for a size 10, adding an extra $\frac{1}{4}$in (5mm) to this measurement for each larger size. This amount includes a $\frac{5}{8}$in (1.5cm) hem allowance.

2 To enable the sleeve cap to fit the enlarged armhole, lower the front and back underarm of the sleeve by $\frac{5}{8}$in (1.5cm). The sleeve must now be made wider: measure out $\frac{3}{8}$in (1cm) from back underarm curve and mark; measure out $\frac{5}{8}$in (1.5cm) on front edge and mark. These amounts include $\frac{3}{8}$in (1cm) for ease on each side of the sleeve cap.

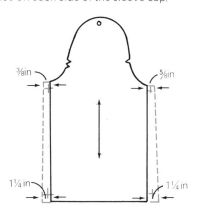

3 At the lower edge, measure out $1\frac{1}{4}$in (3cm) from the cutting line on each side. Connect these points to the marks at the underarm curve for the new underarm cutting line. Mark the seamlines.

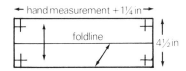

4 To make the cuff pattern, determine the width of the cuff by measuring around the fist and adding $1\frac{1}{8}$in (3cm) to this amount for seam allowance. Draw a rectangle this length by $4\frac{1}{2}$in (11cm) wide. Mark the seam allowance, the foldline through the center, and the grain line parallel to the side edge. The cuff is interfaced to the foldline.

Note As there is no opening in the sleeve, the cuff is joined to form a circle and the hand slipped through, so make allowance for this.

Skirt

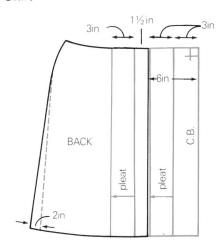

1 To make the skirt back pattern, trace the basic skirt back pattern, leaving extra paper at the center back edge. Omit the dart lines. For the pleat allowance, add 6in (15.5cm) to center back edge. This measurement includes a $\frac{3}{8}$in (1.5cm) seam allowance at new center back line.

2 To mark the pleat position lines, measure off 3, 6, $7\frac{1}{2}$, $10\frac{1}{2}$in (7.5, 15, 19, 26.5cm) from new center back cutting line and mark a series of parallel lines at these points. The first and third lines will be the pleat foldlines and the second and fourth lines will be the pleat position lines (match the foldlines to these to make the pleats).

3 To make the skirt narrower at the lower edge, measure in from the side cutting lines 2in (5cm) and using a yardstick, redraw the side cutting line from the lower edge, tapering into the original cutting line at the hip. Mark the grain line parallel to the center back.

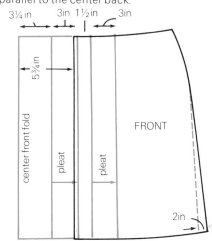

4 To make the skirt front pattern, trace the basic skirt front, leaving extra paper at the center front edge. Omit the dart lines. For the pleat allowance, add $5\frac{3}{4}$in (14.5cm) to the center front edge.

5 To mark the pleat position lines, measure in $3\frac{1}{4}$, $6\frac{1}{4}$, $7\frac{3}{4}$, $10\frac{3}{4}$in (8.5, 16, 20, and 27.5cm) from new center front line and mark a series of parallel lines at these points. The first and third pleat foldlines; the second and fourth are pleat position lines (bring foldlines to meet these).

6 To make the skirt narrower at the lower edge, use the same measurements and directions as for the skirt back (step 3).

Cutting layout for 45in-wide fabric with or without nap

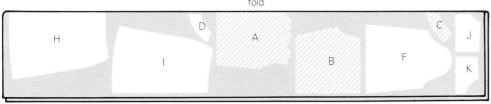

fold

selvages

D A C J
H I B F K

54in-wide fabric with or without nap

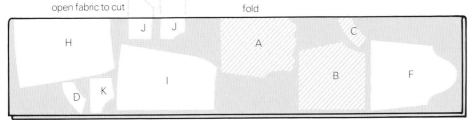

open fabric to cut   fold

J J C
H A
I B F
D K

selvages

36in-wide fabric with nap

fold

E
E G

selvages

36in-wide interfacing

fold

C D
G E

selvages

Directions for making

Suggested fabrics
Medium or lightweight wool plaids, checks, or solids. Crisp polyester and wool blends, linen or rayon blends. Collar and cuffs: velvet, velveteen, linen, cotton pique or poplin.

Materials
45in (115cm)-wide fabric with or without nap:
  Sizes 10, 12: 3$\frac{7}{8}$yd (3.5m)
  Sizes 14, 16: 4yd (3.6m)
  Sizes 18, 20: 4$\frac{1}{8}$yd (3.7m)
54in (140cm)-wide fabric with or without nap:
  Sizes 10, 12: 3$\frac{5}{8}$yd (3.3m)
  Sizes 14, 16: 3$\frac{7}{8}$yd (3.5m)
  Sizes 18, 20: 4yd (3.6m)
36in (90cm)-wide interfacing:
  For all sizes: $\frac{5}{8}$yd (.5m)
Contrasting collar and cuffs
36in (90cm)-wide fabric with or without nap: for all sizes: $\frac{1}{2}$yd (.4m)
Matching thread
Buttonhole twist or embroidery thread for arrowhead tacks
24in (61cm) dress zipper
Hook and eye
Purchased belt

Key to adjusted pattern pieces
A	Front bodice	Cut 1 on fold
B	Back bodice	Cut 2
C	Front neck facing	Cut 1 on fold
D	Back neck facing	Cut 2
E	Collar	Cut 4
F	Sleeve	Cut 2
G	Cuff	Cut 2
H	Skirt front	Cut 1 on fold
I	Skirt back	Cut 2
J	Back yoke	Cut 2
K	Front yoke	Cut 2

Interfacing: use pieces **C** Cut 1 on fold, **D** Cut 2, **E** Cut 2, **G** Cut 2 to half width only.

Note: If working with uneven plaids refer to Volume 7, page 70 for details on preparing the fabric. If using an even plaid, make sure that the bars of upper and under layers of fabric match exactly, and pin the two layers together along selvage to prevent them from slipping when cutting out

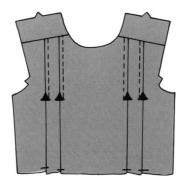

1 Fold and baste the pleats on the front and back bodice. Stitch each pleat, using either the understitching or topstitching method as shown on page 73. Stitch the front pleats 4$\frac{1}{2}$in (11cm) below the yoke seamline and the back pleats 3$\frac{1}{2}$in (9cm) below the yoke seamline. Complete each pleat with an arrowhead tack at the end of the stitching as shown on page 72.
Baste pleats at waist to hold.
2 With right sides together, stitch the the bodice sections. Finish the seam allowances together and press them upward.

3 Fold, baste and stitch the pleats on the skirt front and backs using the same method as on the bodice. Stitch pleats to 6in (15cm) below waist seamline and complete with arrowhead tacks.
4 With right sides together, baste and stitch the center back seam to within 6$\frac{1}{4}$in (16cm) of the waist seamline. Press the seam open.

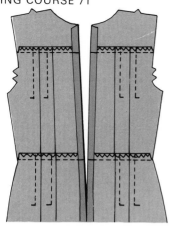

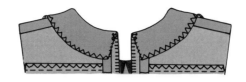

5 With right sides together and the center fronts, center backs and pleats matching, baste and stitch the bodice front to the skirt front and the bodice backs to the skirt backs. Finish the seams together and press upward. Insert zipper into the center back opening as directed for the basic dress (see Volume 4, page 68).

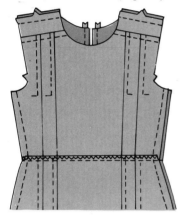

6 With right sides together, baste and stitch the shoulder and side seams. Finish and press seams open.

7 Interface and stitch the two halves of the collar together. Turn right side out and press. Baste to the front and back neck edges, matching center front and center backs.

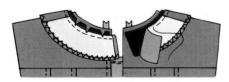

8 Baste the interfacing to the wrong side of the front and back neck facings. With right sides together, baste and stitch the facings together at the shoulder seams. Press seams open. Finish the outer edge of the facings by overcasting or by

turning under $\frac{1}{4}$in (5mm) and machine-stitching. Press.

9 With right sides together and shoulder seams, center fronts and center backs matching, baste and stitch the facings to the neck edge over the collar. Grade and clip the seam allowances.

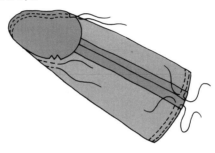

10 Press the seam allowance toward the facing and understitch to prevent rolling. Press. Turn the facings to the inside of the garment and slip stitch to the zipper tape and the center back. Catch-stitch the facing to the shoulder seams. Complete the back neck with a hook and eye.

11 Stitch the underarm seam of the sleeve and press the seam open. Run two rows of gathering stitches around the sleeve cap between the notches and around the lower edge.

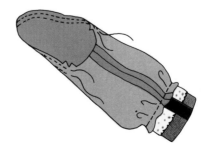

12 Baste the interfacing to half the cuff and catch-stitch to the foldline. With right sides together, baste and stitch the short ends of the cuff together. Trim the interfacing close to the stitching. Press seam open.

13 With right sides together, baste and stitch the cuff to the lower edge of the sleeve, gathering the sleeve to fit the cuff. Trim the seam allowances.
Press the seam allowance toward the cuff.

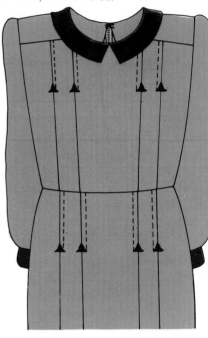

14 On the inside, turn under the seam allowance of the cuff and slip stitch it to the stitching line of the seam. Press carefully on the inside.

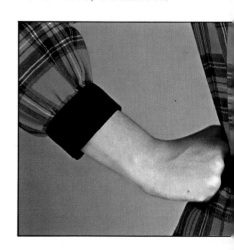

15 Set the sleeve into the armhole as directed for the blouse (see Volume 3, page 59). Turn up the hem of the dress. Baste the pleats in place before giving the hem a final press from the right side.
16 Make a thread belt carrier (see Volume 7, page 67) at each side seam over the waistline for a purchased belt.

sewing / COURSE 72

*Working with knit fabrics
*Applying a cowl-neck collar
 with facings
*Pattern for a two-piece
 suit:
 adapting the pattern;
 directions for making

Working with knit fabrics

The techniques involved in working with knits are similar to those for jersey fabrics, allowing for the fact that knit fabrics are more loosely textured. When preparing the fabric for cutting, it is important to lay the fabric on a surface large enough to prevent the fabric from hanging down over the edge and stretching out of shape. If the fabric has a prominent lengthwise rib, use this as a guide for folding the fabric, and fold it with the right side facing outward.

When pinning the pattern on the fabric,

use fine pins. Use them sparingly and only within the seam allowance. After cutting out, staystitch all curved and bias-cut edges to prevent stretching. If the fabric has a sharply pressed fold, avoid it when you are cutting out the pattern, as it is difficult to press out entirely. When stitching, use synthetic thread and a ball-point needle. A stitched seam must be able to stretch with the fabric, therefore a zig-zag stitch is advisable.

Neckline, shoulder and waist seams usually need seam tape stitched into the

seam to prevent stretching and to support the shape of the garment. If the seam is curved, press the tape into shape before applying it.

To repair a thread which has pulled while you are working, hold the fabric and stretch it along the pulled thread to work as much as possible back into place. Any remaining loose thread can be pushed gently back into the fabric with a tapestry needle.

Before hemming a knit garment, let it hang overnight to drop.

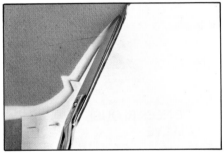
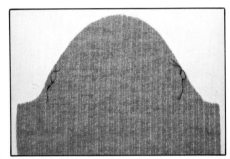

1 If the fabric has a prominent crosswise thread or stripe, treat it in the same way as other striped fabric. Pin the two layers together with the stripe of the top layer matching that of the bottom layer before pinning on pattern.

2 Use sharp scissors for cutting. Cut notches outward on firm knitted fabrics so that they can be matched in the usual way.

3 On loose, open-knit fabrics, mark notches with tailor's tacks. If notches are cut out from fabric, they easily lose definition because of the open stitches.

Applying a cowl-neck collar with facings

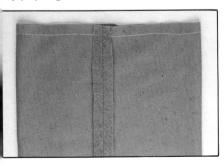
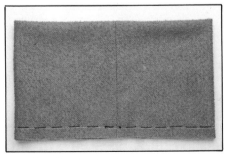
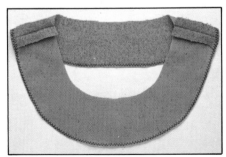

1 Staystitch along both neck edges. With right sides together, baste and stitch the center back seam of collar. Press seam open.

2 With wrong sides together, fold the collar piece in half, bringing the neck edges together. Baste these edges.

3 Join the front and back neck facings together at the shoulder seams. Press seams open. Finish outer raw edge of facings with zig-zag stitch or by turning under $\frac{1}{4}$in (5mm) and machine-stitching.
continued

Simon Butcher

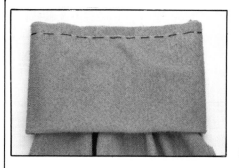

4 Matching the collar seam to the center back neck, pin and baste the collar to the neck edge.

5 With right sides together and seams, center fronts and center backs matching, pin and baste the neck facings to the neck edge over the collar. Stitch around the entire neck edge. Grade and clip the seam allowance.

6 Turn the facings to the inside of the neck edge and baste around the neck. Catch-stitch the facings to the shoulder seams. Press. Remove basting. On the right side, roll the collar downward as shown.

Two-piece suit

This simple outfit is right for almost any occasion – day or night. Make it in knit fabric in a bright jewel color.

Adapting the pattern

The suit is made by adapting the pattern for the basic shirt and the basic skirt from the Stitch by Stitch Pattern Pack, available in sizes 10-20, which correspond to sizes 8-18 in ready-made clothes.

Materials
Two sheets of tracing paper 36×40in (90×100cm)
Flexible curve
Yardstick
Right triangle

Top

Yoke and bodice

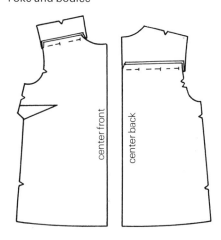

1 Pin the front yoke to the shirt front and

the back yoke to the shirt back, overlapping the ⅝in (1.5cm) seam allowance, so that seamlines are aligned. Trace both pieces, leaving extra paper at the center front and center back.

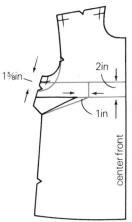

2 On the front pattern, measure 1⅝in (4cm) down side cutting line from lower armhole and mark. Using a flexible curve, connect this point to the notch on the original armhole cutting line.

3 Continue the top bust dart line across to center front edge. Measure 1in (2.5cm) in along this line from the dart point and mark. Redraw the lower bust dart line to meet this point. Using the triangle, measure up 2in (5cm) and draw a line across pattern from side to center for the new yoke line.

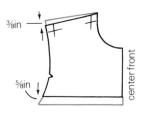

4 Cut along this line to separate the pattern. Add ⅝in (1.5cm) to lower edge of

yoke. Raise shoulder cutting line ⅜in (1cm) at armhole edge and taper the line into the original cutting line at neck edge.

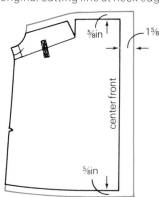

5 On the front bodice, cut down the short line to the new bust point. Close the bust dart and tape it in place. For the gathering allowance add 1⅝in (4cm) to center front edge. Add ⅝in (1.5cm) seam allowance to the top edge of bodice and lengthen the pattern by adding ⅝in (1.5cm) to the lower edge.

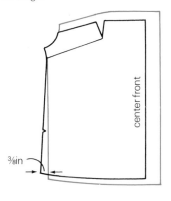

6 Straighten the side seam by measuring ⅜in (1cm) in from side cutting line at lower edge. Redraw the side cutting line from the lower edge up to the cutting line at the armhole.

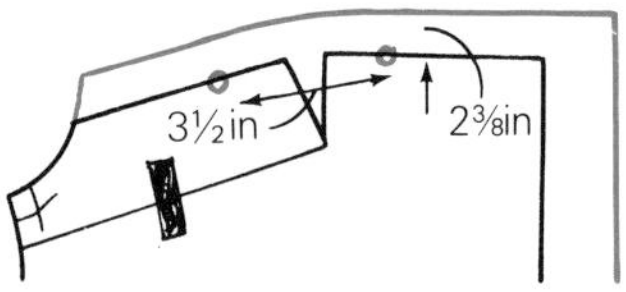

7 For gathering positions, measure in 2⅜in (6cm) along yoke seamline from original center front, then a further 3½in (9cm), and mark these points with circles.

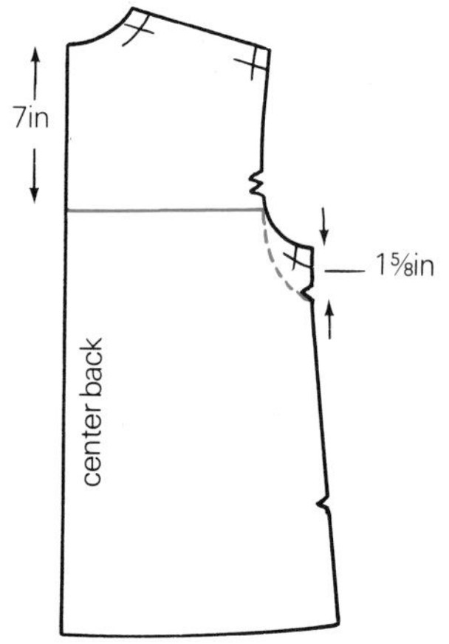

8 Lower the back armhole, using the same measurements and directions as for the front.
For the back yoke line, measure down center back cutting line from back neck 7in (18.5cm) for size 10, adding ¼in (5mm) to this measurement for each larger size, and draw a horizontal line across the pattern.

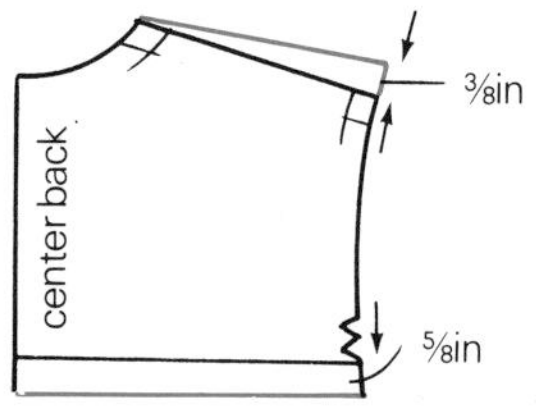

9 To make the yoke pattern, cut along this line to separate the two pieces. Add ⅝in (1.5cm) to lower edge of yoke. Raise shoulder line by ⅜in (1cm) as directed for front yoke.

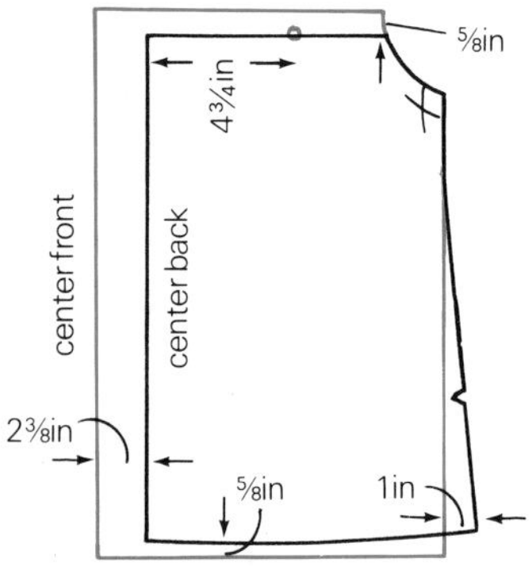

10 For gathering allowance on back bodice, add 2⅜in (6cm) to center back edge. Add ⅝in (1.5cm) seam allowance to top edge and lengthen by ⅝in (1.5cm).

11 Straighten side seam by measuring 1in (2.5cm) in from side edge and drawing the new side cutting line from this point to the armhole edge.
For the gathering position measure in 4¾in (12cm) along yoke line from original center back and mark.

Neckline, facing and collar

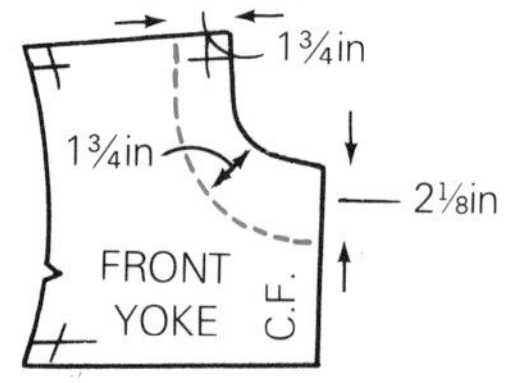

1 On front yoke measure 2⅛in (5.5cm) down center front edge from the neck cutting line and 1¾in (4.5cm) along shoulder seamline. Using a flexible curve, redraw the neck curve by connecting these points. As a guide, the measurement about halfway along the curve will be 1¾in (4.5cm) from the neck edge. Add ⅝in (1.5cm) seam allowance to new neckline before cutting out the pattern.

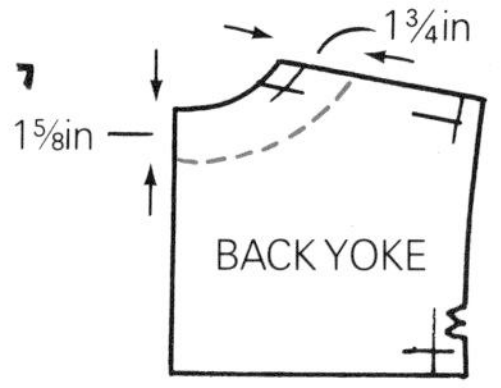

2 On the back yoke measure 1⅝in (4cm) down center back edge from the back neck cutting line and 1¾in (4.5cm) along shoulder seamline. Connect these two points, using a flexible curve. Add ⅝in (1.5cm) seam allowance to the new neckline before cutting out the pattern.

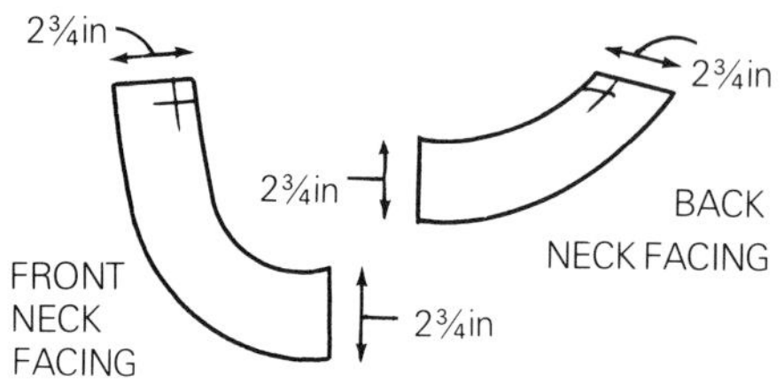

3 Lay tracing paper over the new front and back yokes and trace the necklines. Trace down the center front edge, along shoulder cutting line and down center back to a depth of 2¾in (7cm). Using a flexible curve, draw the outer curved edge of the facings. Mark the seam allowance along neck and shoulder edges.

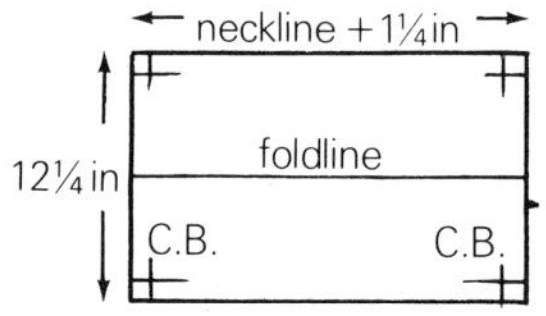

4 To make the collar pattern, determine the length by measuring the finished front and back necklines along the seamlines (excluding seam allowances at shoulder). Add these measurements together and then double the figure. This will be the total neck measurement. Add 1¼in (3cm) for seam allowances. Draw a rectangle for collar pattern to this measurement for length by 12¼in (31cm) wide. Mark the foldline along center of collar.

Sleeve and belt

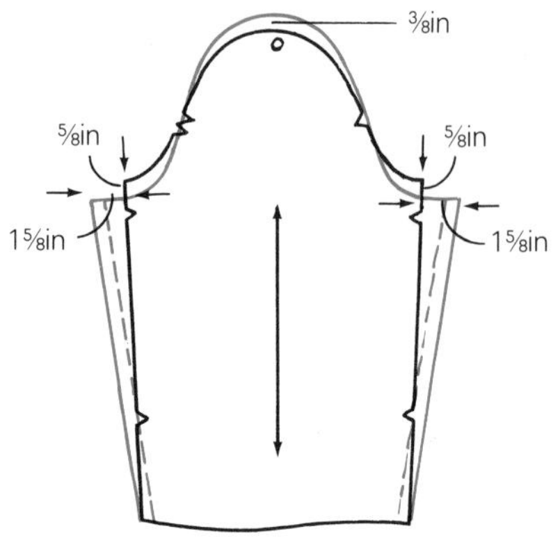

1 Trace the basic sleeve pattern, leaving 8in (20cm) of extra paper at lower edge. Raise center of sleeve cap by ⅜in (1cm). On each side of the sleeve, lower curve at underarm seam by ⅝in (1.5cm), measuring down the underarm cutting line from the cutting line of the curve. From this new point, measure out 1⅝in (4cm) and mark.
Using a flexible curve, redraw the new sleeve cap cutting line as shown, from the top of the sleeve cap to the underarm seamlines. Connect the new point at the underarm to the side cutting line at the lower edge. Mark the seamlines at sleeve cap and underarms.

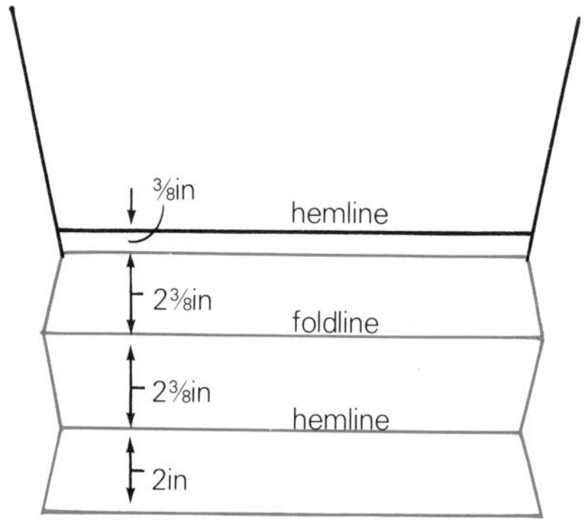

2 Lengthen the sleeve by ⅜in (1cm). Add 2⅜in (6cm), marking this as the foldline; then add another 2⅜in (6cm), marking this as the hemline and a further 2in (5cm) for the facing allowance. Draw a line across the pattern at each measurement.
3 The lower side edges of the sleeve must be shaped to enable the cuff and hem allowance to lie flat against the sleeve.

Fold the cuff and hem allowance in place and trace the side cutting lines along the sides of the cuff. Cut along lines and open out.

4 Cut a pattern piece for the belt backing, following the measurements given in Volume 9, page 61.

Skirt

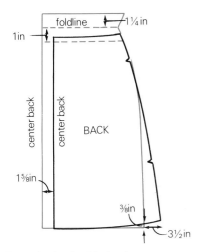

1 Trace the basic skirt back pattern, leaving extra paper at the center back and top edges and omitting waist dart. Add 1⅝in (4cm) to center back edge.

2 For the waistline casing, straighten the waist seamline at the side as shown. Add 1in (2.5cm) to seamline and mark this as casing foldline. Add a further 1¼in (3cm) for facing. Fold the casing downward and shape the side edge, following the side cutting line.

3 At the lower edge, straighten the side seam by measuring 3½in (9cm) in from the side cutting line from this point, tapering into the original line at the hip. Straighten the lower edge by adding ⅜in (1cm) at the side edge, tapering into original cutting line of the hem.

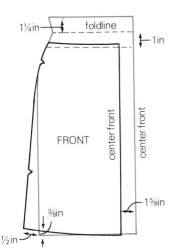

4 Trace the skirt front pattern, leaving extra paper at the center front and top edge. Omit waist dart. Alter the pattern using the same measurements and directions as for the back.

Directions for making

Suggested fabrics
Use a knit fabric that has a slight degree of stretch.

Materials
54in (140cm)-wide fabric with or without nap:
  Sizes 10-14: 4⅛yd (3.7m)
  Sizes 16-20: 4⅜yd (4m)
Matching thread
¾in (2cm)-wide elastic to waist measurement plus 1in (2.5cm)
⅜yd (.3m) seam tape
1½in (4cm)-wide slip buckle
1¼in (3.5cm)-wide belt backing to waist measurement plus 6in (15cm)

Key to adjusted pieces
A	Front yoke	Cut 1 on fold
B	Bodice front	Cut 1 on fold
C	Back yoke	Cut 1 on fold
D	Bodice back	Cut 1 on fold
E	Front neck facing	Cut 1 on fold
F	Back neck facing	Cut 1 on fold
G	Collar	Cut 1
H	Sleeve	Cut 2
I	Skirt back	Cut 1 on fold
J	Skirt front	Cut 1 on fold
K	Belt	Cut 1

Note: When cutting out the pieces for the suit, cut rectangles from the top layer for the front skirt, bodice and yoke, and then fold them in half to cut out. Repeat for the back pieces.

Top

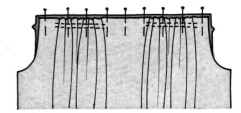

1 Staystitch the front and back neck edges. Run two rows of gathering stitches across the bodice front and back between gathering positions marked on the pattern. With right sides together, pin the front bodice to the front yoke and the back bodice to the back yoke, pulling up the gathering threads until they fit. Baste on the seamline, spreading the gathers evenly.

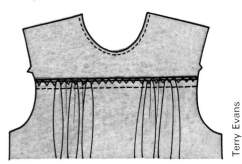

2 Stitch the seams using a method suitable for knits. Remove the basting stitches and finish the seams together with overcasting or zig-zag stitch.

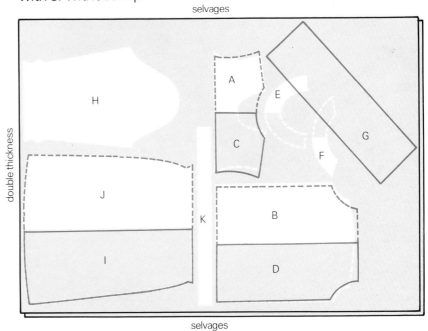

Cutting layout for 54in-wide fabric with or without nap

Note: All the pattern pieces outlined in red are cut out from the bottom layer of fabric. The belt, front neck facing and back neck facing are all cut out once from the top layer of fabric.

Terry Evans

John Hutchinson

3 With right seams together, baste and stitch the shoulder seams using seam tape in the seams as shown in Volume 4, page 61. Stitch, finish and press the side seams.

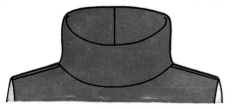

4 Make and apply collar and neck facings as shown on page 79. To complete the neck, turn facings to the inside of the garment and catch-stitch them to the shoulder seams.

5 Mark the foldline at the lower edge of the sleeves with basting. Run two rows of gathering stitches around sleeve cap to ease fullness. With right sides together, baste and stitch the sleeve seams. Finish the seams and press them open.

6 Finish the lower edge of the sleeves. Turn the hem allowance to the inside of the sleeve along the foldline. Baste close to folded edge. Press. Catch-stitch the sleeve hem to the main part of the sleeve. Remove basting.

7 To make the cuff, turn the lower edge of the sleeve back to the right side, folding along the foldline.
Set the sleeves into the armhole as directed for the basic shirt (see Volume 5, page 64). Sew shoulder pads to inside of shoulders as shown in Volume 9, page 6.
8 Turn up the hem and baste close to the folded edge. Finish the raw edge of the hem by overcasting and sew it in place with catch-stitch or herringbone stitch. Remove basting.
9 Make the belt with a slip buckle as explained in Volume 9, page 61, omitting the eyelets. The finished width of the belt will be $1\frac{1}{4}$in (3.5cm).
Try on top and mark the waistline. Make two thread belt carriers, $1\frac{5}{8}$in (4cm) deep, at the side seams.
If you prefer use a ready-made belt; make carriers the same width.

Skirt

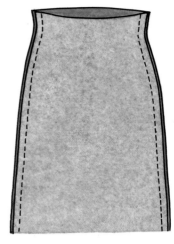

1 With right sides together baste and stitch the side seams of the skirt. Finish and press the seams open.

2 Turn the waistline casing down to the inside along foldline and baste close to the folded edge. Press.

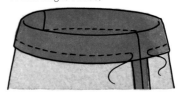

3 To finish the inner edge of the casing turn under $\frac{1}{4}$in (5mm) and stitch casing to skirt close to the inner edge, using a machine stretch stitch. Begin stitching at the side seam and stitch around entire casing, leaving an opening for the elastic to be threaded through.

4 Alternately, finish the raw edge of the casing by overcasting, then machine-stitch the casing to the skirt, stitching $\frac{1}{4}$in (5mm) from the finished edge.
5 Cut a length of elastic to fit comfortably around the waist, plus 1in (2.5cm) seam allowance for joining. Thread elastic through the casing and sew the ends together, overlapping them $\frac{1}{2}$in (1.3cm). Push ends into opening. Press.
6 Turn up the hem using the same method as for the top. If using a bulky fabric, turn under a single layer only. Press lightly from the right side.

Needlework / COURSE 19

*Blackwork
*Some blackwork stitch
  patterns
*Designing blackwork
*A blackwork photograph
  album cover to make

Blackwork

If you enjoy cross stitch, you may find blackwork even more enjoyable. Like cross stitch, it is a form of counted thread embroidery, worked on evenweave fabric, but it uses many different stitch patterns and so can produce more interesting textural contrasts.

Possibly of Spanish origin, blackwork shows the influence of the Moorish civilization which dominated Spain throughout the Middle Ages. Like other forms of Islamic art, Moorish art featured abstract repeating patterns and gracefully interlaced lines, and both of these design elements appeared in the delicate black and white embroidery that became fashionable in 16th-century Spain and then in England. Many portraits of Elizabethan ladies and gentlemen show them wearing clothing adorned with elaborate, swirling blackwork embroidery. Sometimes the work was embellished with gold or silver threads. Blackwork was also extensively used for household linens and hangings. Today blackwork is enjoying a revival. It has a crisp, sophisticated look that appeals to modern taste, and it is much more versatile than it might appear at first glance. You can use the patterns in formal symmetrical designs to decorate table linen or clothing. Or you can use them

pictorially to suggest different textures in a panel or wall hanging, perhaps combining them with free embroidery stitches. You can use colors other than black; red or blue works well on a white or cream background—for a softer effect use cocoa brown on pale beige. You can also reverse the effect by using white or cream thread on a dark fabric. By using different thicknesses of thread you can further increase the textural contrast between the different stitch patterns. And you can create your own patterns, adapting existing ones or starting from scratch.

Materials

The best threads for blackwork are those with a smooth finish, such as *coton à broder* (used for the photo album on page 87), pearl cotton and matte embroidery cotton. For fine work, one or two strands of embroidery floss can be used; for bold effects use fingering or tapestry yarn.

Evenweave cotton and linen are the types of fabric most often used for blackwork. The fewer the number of threads per inch (or centimeter), the smaller and denser a given stitch pattern will be.

Blackwork should be worked in a frame, to facilitate counting the threads and keeping an even tension.

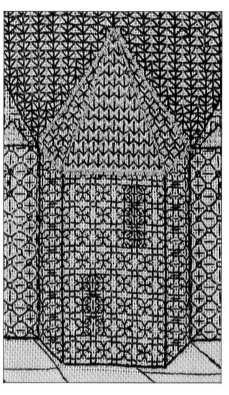

A detail of some contemporary blackwork incorporating gold and silver threads.

Blackwork stitch patterns

All blackwork stitches are based on three simple ones: cross-stitch, back stitch and running stitch. Design areas are usually outlined either in back stitch (see Volume 5, page 76) or in double running, or Holbein stitch, which is worked simply by making a line of even running stitches and then working another line through the same holes, going over the spaces between the original stitches. Outlines can also be worked in couching—a technique to be introduced in a later Needlework course. The filling stitches given here are those used for the photo album cover shown on page 87. Practice them on an extra piece of fabric.

It is best to work small patterns in rows, dividing each stitch into suitable units and working across the fabric. In working larger patterns, such as stitch A, right, complete each motif before moving across to the next.

A (1) The center of this stitch consists of four back stitches, each worked over 4 fabric threads. Each side of the diamond shapes is worked diagonally over 4 vertical and 4 horizontal threads, using back stitch, as shown. The outer "arms" also go over 4 threads.

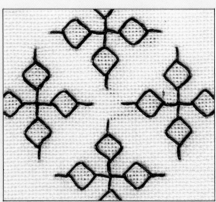

A (2) This sample shows several motifs, spaced as for the album cover design, with 8 fabric threads separating the points of each motif.

Ray Duns

continued

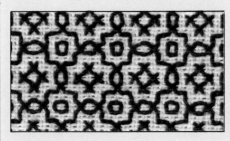

B Each of the individual motifs in this pattern covers 14 vertical and horizontal threads, and each overlaps the adjoining one by 2 threads. Start with the stitches covering the bottom 6 threads. Each individual stitch goes over 2 fabric threads, and the pattern includes backstitch, cross stitch and running stitch.

C This pattern is worked in zig-zag horizontal or vertical rows of alternating boxes and stars. Each box and each star covers 4 horizontal and vertical threads. The "X" inside each box is a cross stitch. The stars consist of a cross stitch with a vertical cross stitch on top.

D This pattern is worked in horizontal or vertical rows. After completing the first row of motifs, go on to the next, positioning the motifs between the first ones as shown. Each motif covers 6 horizontal and vertical threads, and 2 threads separate each motif from the next.

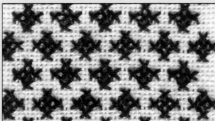

E Work this pattern in rows, starting with the diagonal lines; each zig-zag stitch goes over 4 horizontal and vertical threads. Then fill the spaces with vertical cross stitches over 4 threads, enclosing them in small diamond shapes on alternate rows.

F This pattern is made up entirely of cross stitches, each covering 2 threads, and is best worked in diagonal rows, each motif being completed before you move on to the next.

G This sample illustrates the variation in texture that can be achieved by adding or subtracting parts of the stitch pattern and by using different weights of thread. The main diagonal lines here are straight stitches over 6 vertical and horizontal threads; the small linking squares cover 2 threads.

Designing blackwork

Inspiration for a piece of blackwork can come from many different sources; a still-life painting, a ceramic tile, wallpaper or a brass rubbing, to name just a few. But whatever the source, it's best to convert the original material into a black and white version, the size of the finished work, before choosing the stitches.

We have simplified the process by choosing a black and white photograph as the source of our album cover design. You could, instead, choose a color photo, enlarging it to the correct size and photocopying it. Or, trace the outlines of the print, then fill in the shapes with soft black pencil, making them different shades of gray, corresponding to the intensity of the colors in the original. Obviously, this is a somewhat time-consuming process; and you may well discover that the picture is not really suitable. By starting with a black and white photo, you can instantly see whether or not the picture is a good subject for blackwork. You needn't use the entire picture; you can cut off bits along the edges or use just a small detail—enlarged if necessary.

The next step is to make a tracing of the photo, tracing the main outlines and sim

plifying them where necessary. If you compare the photograph shown here with the trace pattern on page 88, you'll see that the designer has simplified the original photograph considerably, reducing it to a few good strong shapes. The stitches themselves provide detail.

Choosing the stitches is great fun but must be done with care. The scale of the stitch must be suited to the size of the area to be filled; a small area, such as the bell tower, requires a small stitch, so that an adequate number of motifs can be fitted in. Light areas require larger, open patterns: dark areas, dense patterns. Where possible, also try to suit the stitch to the type of object represented. The seemingly curved lines of stitch B, for example, are well suited to the baroque church, whereas the more severe lines of the adjacent buildings are echoed in the mainly horizontal and vertical lines of stitches C and D. In representing the water, the designer has been particularly imaginative; instead of trying to suggest the ripples and reflections (very difficult in counted thread work), she has instead suggested the water's depth, increasing the density of the pattern toward the bottom, to balance the mass of architectural forms.

Souvenir of Venice

A black and white photograph of Venice inspired the blackwork design on this handsome photograph album. You can use our design or make one of your own, using either a black and white or a color print.

Size

The design measures $7\frac{1}{4} \times 6\frac{3}{4}$in (18.5 × 17cm); the album shown measures $11\frac{3}{4} \times 11\frac{1}{2}$in (30 × 29cm).

Materials

Stiff photograph album pages with ready-punched holes—the desired number for the album plus four for the covers

White evenweave cotton or linen with 26 threads to 1in (2.5cm)— enough to cover one side of two album pages plus 2in (5cm) extra all around

White flannelette to fit one side of two album pages

2 skeins of fine coton à broder in black
No. 22 tapestry needle
Embroidery hoop or scroll frame
Needlepoint canvas marker
1yd (1m) of black cord
Stiletto or knitting needle
Artist's spray adhesive
Tracing paper
Felt-tipped pen in a dark color

Working the design

1 Make a tracing of the design on page 88, using a felt-tipped pen; or make and trace your own design (see "Designing blackwork," opposite).

2 From the evenweave fabric cut two pieces to fit the album pages, plus 2in (5cm) extra on all sides.

3 Lay the tracing under one of the pieces of evenweave fabric, placing it equidistant from the top and bottom edges but about $1\frac{1}{2}$in (4cm) closer to the right-hand edge than to the left-hand edge. Make sure that the outer edges of the design are aligned with the fabric threads, and pin the tracing in place.

4 Now trace the design onto the fabric

using the needlepoint marker. (If you have trouble seeing the lines through the fabric, tape it to a window.)

5 Outline the design, including the edges, with backstitch, working each stitch over two fabric threads, or over one for intricate parts of the design.

6 Mount the fabric in the frame. Fill the various design areas with appropriate blackwork stitches. If you are using the design given here, follow the chart and the photographs on pages 85-86. Start with the sky pattern, beginning above the peak of the dome and working from there to left and then to right to fill the space. Then work the smaller patterns. Work the outlines of the water pattern, starting at the lower edge and working upward; then fill in the center motifs.

Assembling the album

1 Press the completed embroidery on the wrong side over a folded towel.

2 If the album pages have a plastic covering, remove this from two of them. These pages will form the front and back covers. Cut two pieces of flannelette to fit the pages and, using spray adhesive, glue them to the outer sides of the two covers. Trim the fabric edges if necessary.

3 Glue the plain piece of evenweave to the back cover, over the flannelette. Trim the edges to about 1 in (2.5cm). Fold them to the wrong side, mitering the corners, and glue them in place.

4 Repeat step 3 for the front cover, first positioning the design carefully so that it is centered between the "hinge" line of the cover and the right-hand edge.

5 To line the covers, use two more album pages. First remove the plastic covering, if any, from the sides to be joined. Then glue the pages to the wrong sides of the covers, aligning the edges and holes.

6 With the stiletto or knitting needle, pierce holes in the fabric on each cover.

7 Insert the remaining pages between the two covers. Thread the cord through the holes and tie the ends together. Knot each end of the cord, trim if necessary and smooth out the threads to form tassels.

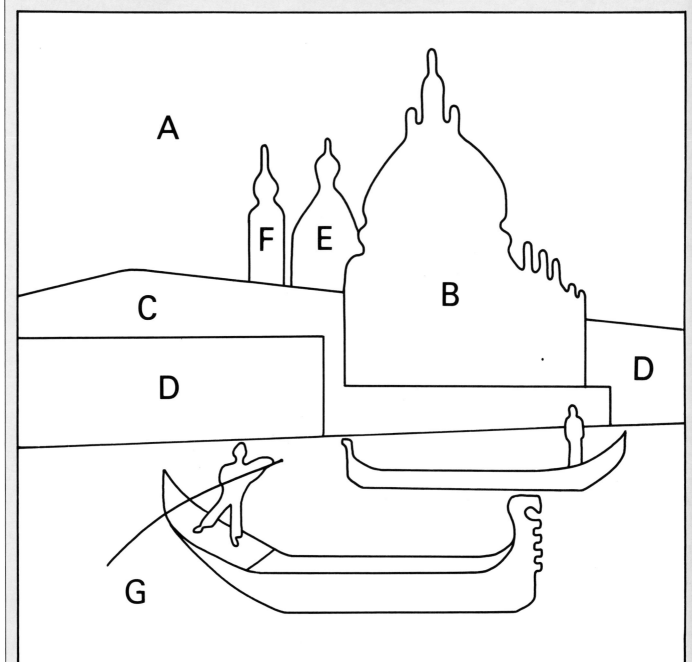

This bright jacket is enhanced by geometric motifs borrowed from Indian designs.

Country style

Sizes To fit 32[34:36:38]in (83[87:92: 97]cm) bust.
Length, 29¾in (73cm).
Sleeve, 19½in (48cm).
Note Directions for larger sizes are in brackets [ ]; if there is only one set of figures it applies to all sizes.

Materials
Knitting worsted
27[29:31:32]oz (750[800:850: 900]g) in main color (A)
8oz (200g) in contrasting color (B)
6oz (150g) in contrasting color (C)
6oz (150g) in contrasting color (D)
4oz (100g) in contrasting color (E)
Sizes G and H (4.50 and 5.00mm) crochet hooks
5 buttons; elastic for cuffs

Gauge

14 sts and 12 rows to 4in (10cm) in hdc patt on size H (5.00mm) hook.

Main part

Using size G (4.50mm) hook and C, make 67ch for side edge.

1st row (RS) 1sc into 2nd ch from hook, 1sc into each ch to end. Turn. 66 sts.
** Join on B.

2nd row With B, work 2ch, 1hdc into each sc to end. Turn.
Join on E.

3rd row Keeping color not in use at wrong side of work, with E work 2ch, 2hdc into sp between first and 2nd hdc, *with B (skip next hdc, 2hdc into next sp between next 2hdc) 3 times, with E skip next hdc, 2hdc into sp between next 2hdc, rep from * to end, finishing with E work 1hdc into last hdc. Turn.

4th row With E 2ch, 2hdc into sp after first 2hdc group, *with B (2hdc into next sp) twice, with E (2hdc into next sp) twice, rep from * to end, finishing last rep with one group in E, with E 1hdc into last hdc. Turn.

5th row With E, 2ch, 1hdc into first sp, 2hdc into next sp, *with B 2hdc into next sp, with E (2hdc into next sp) 3 times, rep from * to end, finishing with 2 groups in E. Turn.
Cut off B.

6th row With E 2ch, 2hdc into each sp to end. Turn.
Cut off E.

7th row With D 2ch, 1hdc into each hdc to within last 2ch. Turn. 66 sts.
Cut off D. Join on A.
Cont in A only. Change to size H (5.00mm) hook.

Patt row 2ch, 1hdc into sp between first and 2nd dc, 1hdc into sp between each hdc to end, working last hdc into sp before 2ch. Turn.
Rep patt row until work measures 15[16:17:18]in (38[41:43:46]cm) from last row in D; end with a WS row.
***Cut off A. Join on E.
Change to size G (4.50mm) hook.

Next row With E 1ch, 1sc into each hdc to end. Turn.
Now rep 2nd to 6th rows inclusive but use C instead of E and D instead of B throughout.

Next row As 7th, using B instead of D.
****

Next row With C 1ch, 1sc into each hdc to end. Turn.
Now rep from* to **** for 2nd half of main part. Fasten off.

Lower border

Using size G (4.50mm) hook and B work a row of sc evenly along one long edge. Turn. Cont in sc, work 1 row D and 1 row C. Fasten off.

Sleeves

Using size G (4.50mm) hook and C, make 67ch. Work as for main part until work measures 15¼in (39cm); end with a WS row. Now work from *** to **** as main part. Fasten off. Join foundation ch and top edge of last row.

Cuffs

Using size G (4.50mm) hook and E work 1sc into each row end around lower edge of sleeve. Cont in hdc working 1 round D, 1 round C and 2 rounds B. Fasten off. Thread elastic through last round.

Yoke

Place a marker at center point of each section in A on top edge of main part for underarm and a marker at center of each section in A on sleeves. Place sleeve markers to markers on main part and join top sleeve edges to top of main part for 6in (15cm) with 3in (7.5cm) each side of marker. Using size G (4.50mm) hook, C and with RS facing, work 27sc across right front edge, 35sc across right sleeve edge, 54sc across back, 35sc across left sleeve and 27sc across left front, turn. 178sts. Join on B and rep 2nd to 7th rows inclusive as main part.

8th row With A 1ch, 1sc into each hdc to end. Turn.

9th row With B 2ch, 1hdc into each of first 2sc, (skip next sc, 1hdc into each of next 3sc) to end. Turn. 134 sts.

10th row With B 2ch, 1hdc into each hdc to end. Turn.

11th row With B 2ch, 2hdc into sp between 2nd and 3rd hdc, *with C skip next hdc, 2hdc into sp between next 2hdc, with B skip next hdc, 2hdc into sp between next 2hdc, rep from * to end. Turn.

12th row With B 2ch, 2hdc into first sp between 2hdc groups, *with C 2hdc into next sp, with B 2hdc into next sp, rep from * to end. Turn.

13th row With B 2ch, with C 2hdc into first sp, *with B 2hdc into next sp, with C 2hdc into next sp, rep from * to end. Turn.

14th row As 13th.

15th row With B 2ch, 2hdc into each sp to end. Turn.

16th row With B 2ch, 1hdc into each of first 4hdc, (skip next hdc, 1hdc into each of next 4hdc) to end. Turn. 108 sts.

17th row With E 1ch, 1sc into each of next 36hdc, (skip next hdc, 1sc into each of next 35hdc) twice. Turn. 106 sts.
Now rep 2nd to 6th rows as main part but work D instead of B and A instead of E throughout.

23rd row With B 2ch, 1hdc into each hdc to end. Turn.

24th row With E 1ch, 1sc into each hdc to end. Turn.

25th row With D 2ch, 1hdc into each of first 6sc, (skip next sc, 1hdc into each of next 2sc) to within last 4sc, 1hdc into each of last 4sc. Turn. 74 sts.

26th row With D 2ch, 1hdc into each hdc to end. Turn.

27th row With D 2ch, 2hdc into sp between 2nd and 3rd hdc, *with C skip next hdc, 2hdc into sp between next 2hdc, with D skip next hdc, 2hdc into sp between next 2hdc, rep from * to end, working last group into sp before 2ch. Turn.

28th row With D 2ch, 2hdc into each sp to end. Turn.

29th row With D 2ch, with C 2hdc into first sp, *with D 2hdc into next sp, with C 2hdc into next sp, rep from * to end. Turn.

30th row As 28th.

31st row With A 2ch, 1hdc into each of first 2hdc, (skip next hdc, 1hdc into each of next 3hdc) to end. Turn. 56 sts.

32nd row With B 1ch, 1sc into each hdc to end. Turn.
Fasten off.

Front borders

Using size G (4.50mm) hook and A, work 2 rows of sc along front edges, making 5 buttonholes on 2nd row on right front yoke by working 3ch, skip next sc for each buttonhole. Press lightly. Sew on buttons.

10¾in

19½in

19in

36[38:40:42]in
all around lower edge

CROCHET

Wrap around

This lacy circular shawl can be worn as a pretty evening wrap. Or work it in one of the pastel shades available to make a very special receiving blanket.

Rod Delroy

91

Size
45¾in (116cm) diameter.

Materials
*Approx 24oz (675g) of a fingering
    yarn
Size C (3.00mm) crochet hook*

Gauge
First 4 rounds measure 5in (13cm) in
diameter.

To make
Using size C (3.00mm) hook make 12ch,
sl st into first ch to form a circle.
1st round 4ch to count as first tr, work
39tr into circle, sl st into top of 4ch.
2nd round 5ch, *1tr into next tr, 1ch,
rep from * all around, sl st into 4th of the
5ch.
3rd round Sl st into first sp, 1sc into same
sp, *5ch, 1sc into next sp, rep from * all
around, finishing 2ch, 1dc into first sc.
4th round *7ch, skip next loop, 1sc into
next loop, (5ch, 1sc into next loop)
twice, rep from * all around finishing 2ch,
1dc into dc of previous round.
5th round *3ch, 3tr, 7ch and 3tr all into
next loop, 3ch, 1sc into next loop, 5ch,
1sc into next loop, rep from * all around,
finishing 2ch, 1dc into dc of previous
round.
6th round 4ch, *15tr all into next 7ch
loop, skip next 3ch sp, 1tr into next
5ch loop, rep from * all around omitting
1tr at end of last rep, sl st into top of the
4ch.
7th round Sl st into next tr, 1sc into next
tr, *(5ch, skip next tr, 1sc into next tr)
6 times, 3ch skip first tr of next 15tr
group, 1sc into next tr, rep from * all
around joining the last 3ch with a sl st to
first sc.
8th round Sl st to center of first loop, 1sc
into same loop, *(5ch, 1sc into next
loop) 5 times, 3ch, skip next 3ch, 1sc
into next 5ch loop, rep from * all around
omitting 1sc at end of last rep, sl st into
first sc.
9th round Sl st to center of first loop, 1sc
into same loop, *(5ch, 1sc into next loop)
4 times, 5ch, skip next 3ch, 1sc into
next 5ch loop, rep from * omitting 1sc at
end of last rep, sl st into first sc.
10th round Sl st to center of next loop,
1sc into same loop, *5ch, 1sc into next
loop, rep from * all around omitting 1sc
at end of last rep, sl st into first sc.
11th round Sl st to center of first loop, 1sc
into same loop, *(5ch, 1sc into next
loop) twice, 6ch, 2sc into next loop, 1sc
into next sc, 2sc into next loop, 6ch,
1sc into next 5ch loop, rep from * omitting
1sc at end of last rep, sl st into first sc.
12th round Sl st to center of first loop, 1sc
into same loop, *5ch, 1sc into next loop,
7ch, 2sc into next loop, 1sc into each of
next 5sc, 2sc into next loop, 7ch, 1sc
into next loop, rep from * all around
omitting 1sc at end of last rep, sl st into
first sc.
13th round Sl st into first loop, 1sc into
same loop, *(7ch, 1sc into same loop)
3 times, 7ch, 3sc into next loop, 1sc
into each of next 9sc, 3sc into next
loop, 7ch, 1sc into next 5ch loop, rep
from * all around omitting 1sc at end of
last rep, sl st into first sc.
14th round Sl st to center of first loop, 1sc
into same loop, *5ch, 1sc into same
loop (1ch, now work 1sc, 5ch and 1sc
all into next loop) twice, 7ch, 1sc into
next loop, 5ch, skip next sc, leaving last
loop of each on hook work 1tr into next
sc, skip next 2sc, 1tr into next sc, (skip
next sc, 1tr into next sc) 3 times, skip
next 2sc, 1tr into next sc, yo and draw
through all loops on hook, 5ch, 1sc into
next loop, 7ch, 1sc into next loop, rep
from *all around finishing 3ch, 1tr into
first sc.
15th round 13ch, *skip next 5ch loop,
1sc into 5ch loop, 10ch, 1dc into next
7ch loop, 10ch, yo, (insert hook into next
loop and draw a loop through) twice,
(yo and draw through first 2 loops on
hook) 3 times, 10ch, 1dc into next 7ch
loop, 10ch, rep from * all around, sl st
into 3rd of the 13ch.
16th round Sl st into first sp, 6ch, (1tr
into first sp, 2ch) 3 times, * into next sp
work (1tr and 2ch) 4 times, rep from *
all around, sl st into 4th of the 6ch.
Rep rounds 3 to 16 inclusive twice more,
then rounds 3 to 6 again. Fasten off.

CROCHET

Bear hugs

A teddy bear adds a touch of fun to a warm bathrobe. Any little girl will love to carry her teddy wherever she goes.

Rod Delroy

93

Sizes

To fit 25[27]in (63[69]cm) chest.
Length, 31[35]in (79[89]cm).
Sleeve seam, 13[15]in (33[38]cm).
Note Directions for larger size are in
brackets []; if there is only one set of
figures it applies to both sizes.

Materials

29[31]oz (800[850]g) of a knitting
  worsted
Teddy bear requires 2oz (50g) of a
  sport yarn
Left-over lengths of black and red
  yarn for nose and bow
Sizes C and G (3.00 and 4.50mm)
  crochet hooks
10[11] buttons; stuffing

Gauge

15dc and 9 rows to 4in (10cm) worked on
size G (4.50mm) hook.

Yoke

Using size G (4.50mm) hook make
37[41]ch.
1st row 1dc into 3rd ch from hook, *2dc
into next ch, 1dc into next ch, rep from *
to within last ch, 1dc into last ch. Turn.
52[58] sts.
2nd row 3ch to count as first dc, 1dc into
next dc, *2dc into next dc, 1dc into each
of next 2dc, rep from * to within last 2 sts,
2dc into next dc, 1dc, 1dc into top of 3ch.
Turn. 69[77] sts.
3rd row 3ch, 1dc into each dc to end.
Turn.
4th row 3ch, 1dc into each of next 2dc,
*2dc into next dc, 1dc into each of next
3dc, rep from * to within last 2 sts, 1dc
into each of next 2dc. Turn. 86[96] sts.
5th row As 3rd.
6th row 3ch, skip first dc, 1dc into each of
next 2dc, *2dc into next dc, 1dc into each
of next 4dc, rep from * to within last 3 sts,
2dc into next st, 1dc into each of last 2 sts.
Turn. 103[115] sts.
7th row As 3rd.
8th row 3ch, 1dc into each of next 3dc,
*2dc into next dc, 1dc into each of next
5dc, rep from * to within last 3 sts, 2dc
into next st, 1dc into each of last 2 sts.
Turn. 120[134] sts.
9th row As 3rd.
10th row 3ch, 1dc into each of next 2dc,
*2dc into next dc, 1dc into each of next
6dc, rep from * to within last 5 sts, 2dc
into next st, 1dc into each of last 4 sts.
Turn. 137[153] sts.
11th row As 3rd.
12th row 3ch, 1dc into each of next 3dc,
*2dc into next dc, 1dc into each of next
7dc, rep from * to within last 5 sts, 2dc into
next dc, 1dc into each of rem 4 sts. Turn.
154[171] sts.
Next row Working into back loop only of
each st, work 1ch, *1sc into each of next
3 sts, 3ch, sl st into last sc worked – picot
formed –, rep from * to end. Fasten off.
Divide for sleeves, back and fronts
Return to beg of last row and working
into front loop only of this row (i.e. the
remainder of sts from picot row) work
3ch, 2dc into each of next 22[24] sts,
make 10[14]ch, skip next 30[34] sts
for sleeve top, then work 2dc into each of

next 48[53] sts, make 10[14] ch, skip
next 30[34] sts, then work 2dc into each
of last 22[24] sts, 1dc into last st. Turn.
Next row 3ch to count as first dc, 1dc into
each dc to ch, 1dc into each ch, 1dc into
each dc across back, 1dc into each ch,
then 1dc into each dc to end. Turn.
206[232] sts.
Next row 3ch, 1dc into each dc to end.
Turn.
Rep last row until work measures 31[35]
in (79[89]cm) (or desired length).
Fasten off.

Sleeves (alike)

With RS facing rejoin yarn to 6th[8th]
ch at underarm, 3ch, 1dc into each
of next 4[6] ch, then 1dc into each
of the 30[34] free sts on yoke, 1dc into
each of rem 5[7] ch at underarm. Turn.
40[48] sts.
Next row 3ch, 1dc into each dc to end,
1dc into top of 3ch. Turn.
Rep last row until sleeve measures
11[13]in (28[33]cm).
Cuff
Next row 1ch, *(insert hook into next st,
yo and draw a loop through) twice, yo
and draw through all loops on hook, rep
from * to end. Turn. 20[24] sts.
Next row 1ch, 1sc into each sc to end.
Turn. Rep last row until cuff measures
2in (5cm). Fasten off.

Button band

Using size G (4.50mm) hook and with RS
facing join yarn to first row end of left
front yoke at neck edge and work 1ch,
2sc into same row end, *1sc into next
row end, 2sc into next row end, rep from
* to lower edge, turn.
Next row 1ch, 1sc into each sc to end.
Turn.
Rep the last row 3 times more. Fasten off.
Buttonhole band
Using size G (4.50mm) hook and with RS
facing join yarn to last row end of lower
edge of right front and work 1ch, 2sc
into same row end, *1sc into next row
end, 2sc into next row end, rep from
* to neck edge, turn.
Next row 1ch, 1sc into each of first 2sc,
*2ch, skip next 2sc, 1sc into each of
next 6sc, rep from * along front edge,
making sure that the last buttonhole is
approx 2¾-4in (7-10cm) from the lower
edge. Turn.
Next row 1ch, 1sc into each sc and 2sc
into each 2ch sp to end. Turn.
Work 2 more rows in sc.
Fasten off.
Sew on buttons to correspond with
buttonholes.
Pockets (make 2)
Using size G (4.50mm) hook make 17ch.
1st row 1sc into 2nd ch from hook, 1sc
into each ch to end. Turn. 16sc.
2nd row 1ch, 1sc into each sc to end.
Turn. Rep 2nd row until pocket measures
4¾in (12cm). Fasten off.

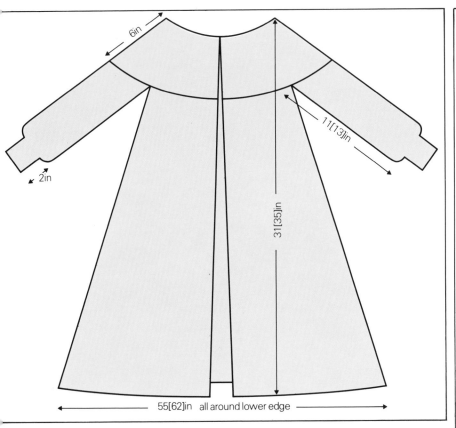

6in

2in

11[13]in

31[35]in

55[62]in all around lower edge

To finish
Sew one pocket to each front in position desired. Using size G (4.50mm) hook work 1sc in each st all around neck edge. Fasten off. Join underarm seams.

Teddy bear
Head
Using size C (3.00mm) hook and main color make 4ch, sl st into first ch to form a circle.

1st round 8sc into circle.
2nd round 1sc into each sc all around.
3rd round As 2nd.
4th round 2sc into each sc all around. 16sc.
5th round 1sc into each sc all around.
6th round *1sc into next sc, 2sc into next sc, rep from * all around. 24sc.
7th round As 5th.
8th round *1sc into each of next 2sc, 2sc into next sc, rep from * all around.
9th round As 5th.
10th round *1sc into each of next 3sc, 2sc into next sc, rep from * all around. 40sc.
11th round As 5th. Fasten off.

Body
Using size C (3.00mm) hook make 4ch, sl st to first ch to form a circle.

1st round 8sc into circle.
2nd round 2sc into each sc. 16sc.
3rd round *2sc into next sc, 1sc into next sc, rep from * all around. 24 sts.
4th round 1sc into each sc all around.
5th round *2sc into next sc, 1sc into each of next 2sc, rep from * all around.

6th round As 4th.
7th round *2sc into next sc, 1sc into each of next 3sc, rep from * all around. 40sc.
8th round As 4th.
9th round *2sc into next sc, 1sc into each of next 4sc, rep from * all around. 48 sts.
10th round As 4th. Fasten off.

Arms
Using size C (3.00mm) hook make 4ch, sl st into first ch to form a circle.
1st round 8sc into circle.
2nd round 2sc into each sc. 16sc.
3rd round 1sc into each sc all around.
Rep 3rd round 9 times. Fasten off.

Legs
Work as for arms but rep 3rd round 13 times.

Ears
Make 3ch, sl st into first ch to form a circle.
1st round 8sc into circle.
2nd round 2sc into each sc. 16sc.
3rd round *1sc into next sc, 2sc into next sc, rep from * all around. 24sc. Fasten off.

To finish
Attach head and body to bathrobe yoke, stuffing as you sew. Stuff arms and legs and attach to body. Sew on ears.
Bow
Using size C (3.00mm) hook and red yarn double, make a ch of approx 12in (30cm). Tie in a bow and attach to neck.

Technique tip
Three-dimensional motifs

Motifs can be worked, padded and sewn to garments to give a three-dimensional appearance. The teddy bear motif on the bathrobe is worked in separate pieces and then sewn to the yoke, with the stuffing inserted at the same time.

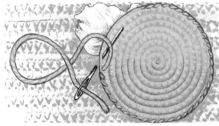

Crochet each piece as instructed. Sew body to yoke, overcasting around outer edge and inserting stuffing as you sew.

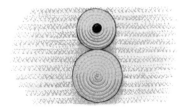

Embroider the nose in center of face, then sew on face, stuffing as you sew, joining it to body at lower section.

The arms and legs are made from tubular pieces. Stuff each piece, join the top edge and sew the arms and legs to body so that they hang.

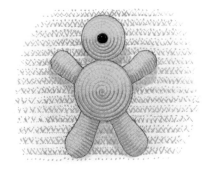

The padded pieces of crochet look far more interesting than flat pieces of crochet. Once the padded pieces have been attached, the remaining features can be added.

Coral Mula

Lord of the Isles

This magnificent Fair Isle jacket is knitted in pure wool—choose from the range of colors shown here. And we've trimmed the raglan seams with spool knitting to add a special touch.

Sizes
To fit 34-36[38-40]in (87-92[97-102]cm) chest.
Length, 23¾[24¼]in (60[61]cm).
Sleeve seam, 19½in (49cm).

Note: Directions for larger size are in brackets []; if there is only one set of figures it applies to both sizes.

Materials
13[15]oz (350[400]g) of a sport yarn in main color
2oz (50g) in each of 3 contrasting colors (A, B and C)
1oz (25g) in each of 4 contrasting colors (D, E, F and G)
Nos. 2 and 3 (3 and 3¼mm) knitting needles
10 buttons
Knitting spool

Gauge
28 sts and 36 rows to 4in (10cm) in Fair Isle patt worked on No. 3 (3¼mm) needles.

Back
Using No. 2 (3mm) needles and main color cast on 88[104] sts. Work in stockinette st for 4½in (12cm); end with a K row.
Inc row (Inc in next st, P1) to end. 132[156] sts. Change to No. 3 (3¼mm) needles. Reading RS rows from right to left and WS rows from left to right, cont in Fair Isle patt from chart until work measures 18in (46cm); end with a WS row.

Shape raglan armholes
Bind off 3 sts at beg of next 2 rows. Dec one st at each end of next and every foll alternate row until 66[102] sts rem, then dec one st at each end of every row until 42[46] sts rem. Cut off yarn and leave sts on a holder.

Left front
Using No. 2 (3mm) needles and main color, cast on 40[48] sts. Work in stockinette st for 4½in (12cm); end with a K row.
Inc row (Inc in next st, P1) to end. 60[72] sts. Change to No. 3 (3¼mm) needles. Reading RS rows from right to left and WS rows from left to right, cont in Fair Isle patt from chart until work measures 7½in (19cm); end with a P row.
Divide for pocket
Next row Patt 26[32], turn and leave rem sts on a spare needle.
Cont in patt on these sts until work measures 13in (33cm); end at inner edge. Cut off yarn and leave sts on a spare needle.
Join yarn to inner end of first set of sts on spare needle and patt to end of row. Cont in patt until work measures 13in (33cm); end at outer edge.
Next row Patt to end, then onto same needle patt the sts of first side. 60[72] sts. Cont in patt until front is same length as back to raglan; end with a P row to match back.
Shape raglan armhole
Bind off 3 sts at beg of next row. Dec one st at beg of every foll alternate row until 27[45] sts rem, then dec one st at

Peter Waldman/Designed by Sandy Black

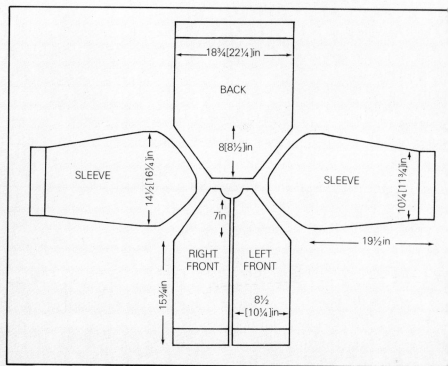

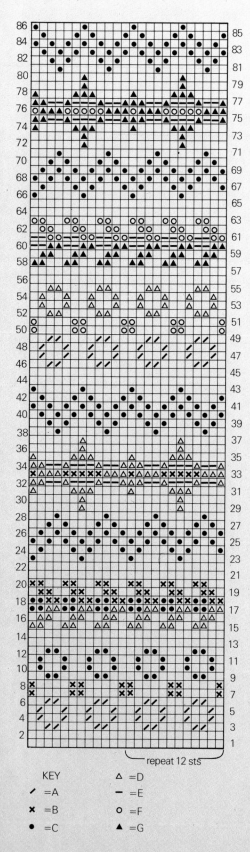

The chart rows are numbered on the left side 2, 4, 6, 8, 10, 12, 14, 16, 18, 20, 22, 24, 26, 28, 30, 32, 34, 36, 38, 40, 42, 44, 46, 48, 50, 52, 54, 56, 58, 60, 62, 64, 66, 68, 70, 72, 74, 76, 78, 80, 82, 84, 86 and on the right side 1, 3, 5, 7, 9, 11, 13, 15, 17, 19, 21, 23, 25, 27, 29, 31, 33, 35, 37, 39, 41, 43, 45, 47, 49, 51, 53, 55, 57, 59, 61, 63, 65, 67, 69, 71, 73, 75, 77, 79, 81, 83, 85.

repeat 12 sts

KEY

✔	=A	△	=D
✕	=B	−	=E
●	=C	○	=F
		▲	=G

raglan edge on every row until 25[31] sts rem, so ending at front edge.

Shape neck
Cont to dec at raglan edge on every row, bind off 7 sts at beg of next row, then dec one st at neck edge on every row until 7[9] sts rem. Cont to dec at raglan edge only until 3 sts rem. Bind off.

Right front
Work as for left front, reversing all shaping and position pocket thus:
Next row K34[40], turn and leave rem sts on a spare needle.

Right sleeve
Using No. 2 (3mm) needles and main color, cast on 41[52] sts. Work in stockinette st for 4½in (12cm); end with a K row.
Inc row P0[1], * P1, (inc in next st) 4[2] times, rep from * to last 6 sts, P1 (inc into next st) 3[2] times, P2[3]. Change to No. 3 (3¼mm) needles. Reading RS rows from right to left and WS rows from left to right, cont in Fair Isle patt from chart inc one st at each end of every 9th row until there are 102[114] sts. Cont straight until work measures 19½in (49cm) from beg; end with a P row.
Shape raglan armhole
Bind off 3 sts at beg of next 2 rows. Dec one st at each end of every other row until 56[72] sts rem. Cont to shape left edge in this way, at right edge dec one st on every row 10 times, then dec one st at each end of every row until 3 sts rem. Bind off. Mark 13th row down from bound-off edge on the right-hand edge with a colored thread.

Left sleeve

As right sleeve, reversing top shaping.
Pocket borders and linings (alike)
With RS facing, join on main color and using No. 2 (3mm) needle pick up and K 44 sts along front edge of pocket opening. Beg with a P row, work in stockinette st for 10¼[11¼]in (26[28.5] cm). Bind off.

Buttonhole border
With RS facing join on main color and using No. 2 (3mm) needle pick up and K 185 sts evenly along front edge to center of waistband. Beg with a P row work 3 rows stockinette st.
1st buttonhole row K5, bind off 3, (K unti there are 16 sts on right-hand needle afte binding off, bind off 3) 9 times, K to end.
2nd buttonhole row P to end, casting on 3 sts over those bound off on previous row. Work 10 rows stockinette st, work 2 buttonhole rows, then work 4 rows stockinette st. Bind off.
Button border
Work as for buttonhole border, omitting buttonholes

Collar
With RS facing, join main color to beg of right front neck and using No. 2 (3mm) needle pick up and K 16[20] sts along front neck, 9 sts from colored thread on right sleeve, 42[46] sts across back neck, 9 sts from left sleeve to colored thread and 16[20] sts across left front neck. 92[104] sts. P 1 row.
Next 6 rows Work to last 3 sts, turn.
Next 6 rows Work to last 4 sts, turn.
Next 8 rows Work to last 5 sts, turn.
Work 2 rows across all sts, then work turning rows in reverse order. Work 1 row across all sts. Bind off loosely.

Sleeve trimming

Using main color, work four 14¼in (36cm) lengths of spool knitting.

To finish

Press or block, according to yarn used. Join raglan seams, then join side and sleeve seams. Fold cuffs, waistband, borders and collar to WS and slip stitch in position. Allow 1in (2.5cm) for pocket border, then sew pocket linings in place. Finish buttonholes and sew on buttons. Sew piping along raglan seams.

Technique tip

Spool knitting

Use a block or cylinder of wood with a ¼in (1cm)-diameter hole through center. Hammer four small nails at regular intervals around the center hole. Thread end of ball of yarn down through hole; hold in place with left hand while working.

Wind yarn, in counterclockwise direction around each nail as shown.

Working in clockwise direction, take yarn around outer edge of next nail and, using a tapestry needle, lift the lower loop up over the yarn and over the nail.

Continue working around each nail in this way, working in a continuous circle to form a tubular cord. To bind off, pass each loop over next nail in clockwise direction. When 1 loop remains cut off yarn, pass end through last loop and pull up firmly.

Terry Evans

EXTRA SPECIAL KNITTING

Headline news

Make the front page in this dramatic top and jacket.

Sizes
To fit 32[34:36:38]in (83[87:92:97]cm) bust.
Sleeveless top length, $21\frac{1}{2}$[$21\frac{3}{4}$:$22\frac{1}{4}$: $22\frac{3}{4}$]in (53.5[54:55.5:56]cm).
Jacket length, $20\frac{3}{4}$[$21\frac{1}{4}$:$21\frac{3}{4}$:$22\frac{1}{4}$]in (52.5[54:55.5:56.5]cm).
Sleeve seam, $17\frac{1}{2}$[$17\frac{1}{2}$:18:18]in (44.5[44.5:46:46]cm).
Note Directions for larger sizes are in brackets []; if there is only one set of figures it applies to all sizes.

Materials
Sleeveless top 5[5:6:6]oz (120[120: 140:140]g) of a sport yarn in white
3[3:4:4]oz (80[80:100:100]g) in black
Nos. 2 and 3 (3 and $3\frac{1}{4}$mm) knitting needles
Jacket 17[18:20:21]oz (480[500: 540:560]g) of a sport yarn in white
Nos. 5 and 6 (4 and $4\frac{1}{2}$mm) knitting needles
Cable needle; 1 button; snap

Gauge
Top 28 sts and 36 rows to 4in (10cm) in stockinette st on No. 3 ($3\frac{1}{4}$mm) needles.
Jacket 30 sts and 32 rows to 4in (10cm) in patt on No. 6 ($4\frac{1}{2}$mm) needles.

Sleeveless top

Back
Using No. 3 ($3\frac{1}{4}$mm) needles and white, cast on 103 sts for side edge. Beg with a K row, work 6[4:4:4] rows stockinette st. Join in black. Cont in stripe sequence of 6 rows each of black and white throughout, work 0[0:2:2] rows.
Shape armhole
Inc one st at beg of next row and end of foll row. Rep last 2 rows twice more. Cast on 38[40:44:46] sts at beg of next row. 147[149:153:155] sts.
Shape shoulder
Inc one st at beg of every foll 6th row 6 times in all. 153[155:159:161] sts. ** Work 2[4:6:10] rows straight. Place a marker at shoulder edge on last row. Work another 48[56:60:64] rows straight. Place a marker at shoulder edge on last row.
***Work 2[4:6:10] rows straight.
Shape shoulder
Dec one st at shoulder edge on next and every foll 6th row 6 times in all.

147[149:153:155] sts. Work 5 rows straight.
Shape armhole
Next row P to last 38[40:44:46] sts, bind off these sts.
With RS facing, rejoin yarn to rem sts. Dec one st at armhole edge on next 6 rows, 103 sts. Work 6[4:6:6] rows straight, so ending with 6[4:2:2] rows white. Bind off.

Front
Work as for back to **. Work 1[3:5:9] rows straight.
Shape neck
Bind off 11[11:13:13] sts at beg of next row, then dec one st at neck edge on next 12 rows. Work 23[31:35:39] rows straight. Inc one st at neck edge on next 12 rows. Cast on 11[11:13:13] sts at beg of next row.
Complete as for back from ***.

Neckband
Join left shoulder seam. Using No. 2 (3mm) needles, white and with RS facing, pick up and K 40[40:44:46] sts across back neck between markers and 58[60:68:72] sts evenly from front neck edge, 98[100:112:118] sts. Work 8 rows K1, P1 ribbing. Beg with a K row, work 6 rows stockinette st. Cut off white. Join in black. Work 5 rows stockinette st. Bind off knitwise.
Armhole edging
Join right shoulder and neckband seams. Using No. 2 (3mm) needles, white and with RS facing, pick up and K 96[98:102: 106] sts evenly around armhole edge. Beg with a P row, work 3 rows stockinette st inc 1 st at each end of every row. Bind off.
Lower edging
Using No. 2 (3mm) needles, white and

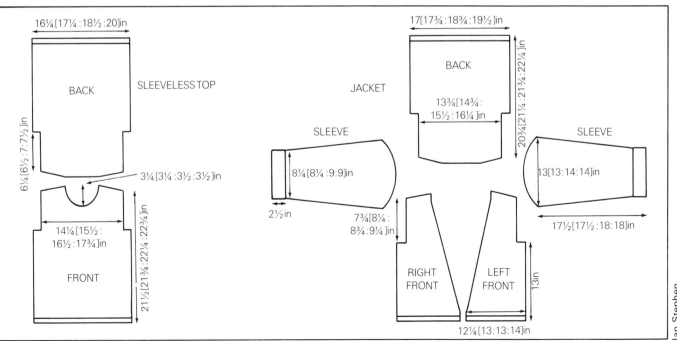

SLEEVELESS TOP
$16\frac{1}{4}$[$17\frac{1}{4}$:$18\frac{1}{2}$:20]in
BACK
$6\frac{1}{4}$[$6\frac{1}{2}$:7:$7\frac{1}{2}$]in
$3\frac{1}{4}$[$3\frac{1}{4}$:$3\frac{1}{2}$:$3\frac{1}{2}$]in
FRONT
$14\frac{1}{4}$[$15\frac{1}{2}$: $16\frac{1}{2}$:$17\frac{3}{4}$]in
$21\frac{1}{2}$[$21\frac{3}{4}$:$22\frac{1}{4}$:$22\frac{3}{4}$]in

JACKET
17[$17\frac{3}{4}$:$18\frac{3}{4}$:$19\frac{1}{2}$]in
BACK
$13\frac{3}{4}$[$14\frac{3}{4}$: $15\frac{1}{2}$:$16\frac{1}{4}$]in
$20\frac{3}{4}$[$21\frac{1}{4}$:$21\frac{3}{4}$:$22\frac{1}{4}$]in
SLEEVE
$8\frac{1}{4}$[$8\frac{1}{4}$:9:9]in
$2\frac{1}{2}$in
$7\frac{3}{4}$[$8\frac{1}{4}$: $8\frac{3}{4}$:$9\frac{1}{4}$]in
RIGHT FRONT
LEFT FRONT
13in
$12\frac{1}{4}$[13:13:14]in

SLEEVE
13[13:14:14]in
$17\frac{1}{2}$[$17\frac{1}{2}$:18:18]in

Ian Stephen

with RS facing, pick up and K 106[108: 112:116] sts evenly from row ends at lower edge of front. Work 3 rows K1, P1 ribbing. Bind off in ribbing. Work along lower edge of back in same way.

To finish

Press or block, according to yarn used. Join side and edging seams. Turn armhole edgings to WS and sew bound-off edge in place on inside. Fold neckband to RS so that stockinette st section is on outside and sew bound-off ridge in place on RS. Press seams.

Jacket

Back

Using No. 5 (4mm) needles cast on 120[126:132:138] sts. Work 6 rows K1, P1 ribbing.
Inc row Rib 7[10:13:16], *inc in next st, rib 14, rep from *6 times, inc in next st, rib 7[10:13:16]. 128[134:140:146] sts.
Change to No. 6 (4½mm) needles. Beg patt.
1st row (WS) K1, *K2, P4, rep from * to last st, K1.
2nd row K1, *sl next 2 sts onto cable needle and leave at front of work, K2, then K2 from cable needle, P2, rep from * to last st, K1.
3rd row As first.
4th row K1, P2, *K2, sl next 2 sts onto cable needle and leave at back of work, K2, then P2 from cable needle, rep from * to last 5 sts, K5.
5th row K1, *P4, K2, rep from * to last st, K1.
6th row K1, *P2, sl next 2 sts onto cable needle and leave at back of work, K2, then K2 from cable needle, rep from * to last st, K1.
7th row As 5th.
8th row K5, *sl next 2 sts onto cable needle and leave at front of work, P2, then K2 from cable needle, K2, rep from * to last 3 sts, P2, K1.
These 8 rows form patt. Cont in patt until work measures 13in (33cm); end with a WS row.
Shape armholes
Bind off 12 sts at beg of next 2 rows. 104[110:116:122] sts.
Cont straight until armhole measures 7¾[8¼:8¾:9¼]in (19.5[21:22.5:23.5]cm); end with a WS row.
Shape shoulders
Bind off 8[8:9:9] sts at beg of next 6 rows and 6[8:8:10] sts at beg of foll 2 rows. Leave rem 44[46:46:48] sts on a holder.

Left front

Using No. 5 (4mm) needles cast on 86[92:92:98] sts. Work 6 rows K1, P1 ribbing.
Inc row Rib 10[13:13:16], *inc in next st, rib 12, rep from * 4 times, inc in next st, rib 10[13:13:16]. 92[98:98:104] sts.

Change to No. 6 (4½mm) needles. Work 8 rows patt as for back.
Shape front edge
Keeping patt correct, dec one st at front edge on next and every foll 3rd row until work measures same as back to armhole; end at side edge.
Shape armhole
Bind off 12 sts at beg of next row. Keeping armhole edge straight, cont to dec one st at front edge only on every 3rd row until 30[32:35:37] sts rem. Cont straight until work measures same as back to shoulder; end at armhole edge.
Shape shoulder
Bind off 8[8:9:9] sts at beg of next and foll 2 alternate rows. Work 1 row. Bind off rem 6[8:8:10] sts.

Right front
Work as left front, reversing shaping.

Sleeves
Using No. 5 (4mm) needles cast on 42[42:44:44] sts. Work 2½in (6.5cm) K1, P1 ribbing.
1st and 2nd sizes only
Inc row Rib 2, *inc in next st, rib 1, rep from *'19 times. 62 sts.
3rd and 4th sizes only
Inc row Rib 1, *inc in next st, rib 1, rep from * 8 times, inc in each of next 6 sts, **rib 1, inc in next st, rep from ** 8 times, rib 1. 68 sts.
All sizes
Change to No. 6 (4½mm) needles. Work 8 rows patt as for back. Keeping patt correct and working extra sts into patt, inc one st at each end of next and every foll 8th row until there are 72[74:80:82] sts, then on every foll 4th row until there are 98[98:104:104] sts. Cont straight until sleeve measures 17½[17½:18:18]in (44.5[44.5:46:46]cm); end with a WS row. Place a marker at each end of last row. Patt a further 10 rows straight.
Shape top
Bind off 4 sts at beg of next 14 rows. Bind off rem sts.
Front edging
Using No. 5 (4mm) needles and with RS facing, pick up and K 128[133:137:141] sts evenly from row ends of one front. K 2 rows. Bind off knitwise. Work other front edging in same way.
Back neck edging
Using No. 5 (4mm) needles and with RS facing work across back neck sts:
Next row K3[4:4:5], *K2 tog, K5, rep from * 4 times, K2 tog, K4[5:5:6]. K 2 rows. Bind off knitwise.

To finish
Press or block, according to yarn used. Join shoulder seams. Set in sleeves, sewing row ends above markers to bound-off sts at underarm. Join side and sleeve seams. Make a loop at lower point of right front edge. Sew button to left front and snap to underlap.

Technique tip

Button loops

Button loops are a neat form of fastening that can be worked on the edge of a garment. Here are two types of button loops: the first is a length of crochet chain; the second, strands of yarn bound with buttonhole stitch.
To work a chain button loop, attach yarn to edge of garment and, using a crochet hook, work a length of chain for the size of button loop required, then slip stitch into the edge of the fabric, making sure that there is enough space for the button to pass through. Fasten off. Sew in ends.

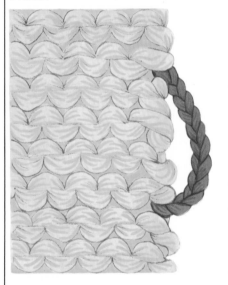

To work a bound button loop, thread a tapestry needle with yarn, secure yarn on wrong side of garment, bring needle through to right side and work a small stitch at opposite end, leaving a loop of required length. Now work a small stitch at starting point, leaving a loop of same size. Work buttonhole stitch over the loops as shown.

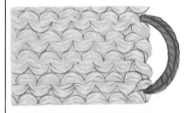

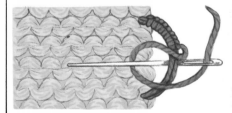

EXTRA SPECIAL SEWING

The allure of the East

These evening outfits have a flavor of the Orient about them. The bodice drapes from pleats at the shoulder which are echoed in the cummerbund. The outfit can be made with a flared skirt or with harem pants.

Measurements

To fit sizes 10[12:14].
Finished back length of long skirt from waistline, 43½in (110cm); finished side length of pants from waistline, 45¼in (115cm) (to allow for blousing at ankle).

Suggested fabrics

Crepe, voile.

Note: Measurements are for size 10; sizes 12 and 14 follow in brackets []. If only one figure is given it applies to all sizes. ⅝in (1.5cm) seam and hem allowances are included. ¾in (2cm) allowances provided at waist for casing.

Dress

Materials

7¾yd (7m) of 36in (90cm)-wide
  fabric or 5¼yd (4.8m) of 60in
  (150cm)-wide fabric
14in (35cm) dress zipper
Nine hooks and eyes
⅞yd (.8m) of ⅜in (1cm)-wide elastic
3in (7.5cm) of ⅜in (1cm)-wide tape
Matching thread, paper for pattern
Yardstick, flexible curve

1 For an accurate fit it is advisable to make a paper pattern for each piece before cutting out, following the measurement diagrams overleaf. Trace the front facing, following the cutting line given on the bodice and mark the grain line as shown. Before cutting out, check skirt length and adjust if necessary. Following the appropriate cutting layout cut out all the pieces.
Note: Bodice and cummerbund are cut on the bias.
2 Mark notches on bodice to show position of pleats, center front and back and right side seams. On cummerbund, mark solid lines and broken lines with rows of tailor's tacks in different colors to show position of pleats.

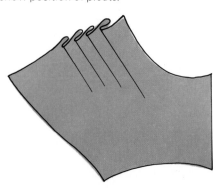

3 To make shoulder pleats on bodice back and front, bring notches together along shoulder edge, working from the right side and starting with the first notch 2¾in (7cm) in from neck edge. Check that pleats are 1in (2.5cm) deep on right side and 1in (2.5cm) apart. Baste in place.
4 With right sides together pin, baste and stitch front to back at shoulder seam, checking that pleats match at seam line. Press seam open and finish.
5 With right sides together, join the two facing sections together at shoulder seam. Trim allowances and press open. Finish outer edge of facing.

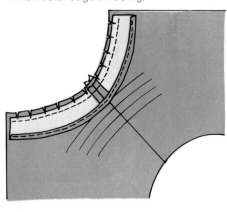

6 With right sides together, pin, baste and stitch facing to neck edge of bodice, matching shoulder seams. Trim seam allowances and clip into curve.

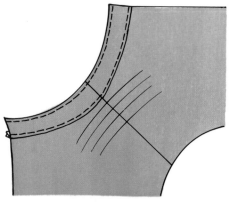

7 Press allowances toward facing. Working from the right side understitch the facing close to the seamline. Press on wrong side and catch in place at shoulder seam by sewing facing to seam allowance.

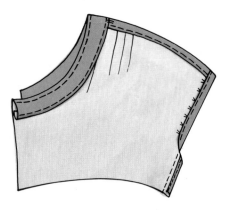

8 With right sides together, baste, pin, and stitch front to back at right side seam, ending stitching at notch above waist. Press open and finish. Turn under hem around sleeve edge and slip stitch in place.

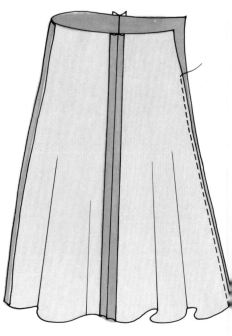

9 With right sides together, pin, baste, and stitch all four skirt sections together at side seams, leaving a 7in (18cm) opening at waist on left side for zipper.

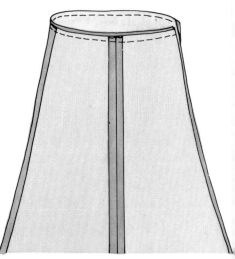

10 With right sides together, slip bodice inside skirt and seam, matching side seams and center front and back and easing in skirt fullness. Baste and stitch seam, taking a ¾in (2cm) seam allowance.

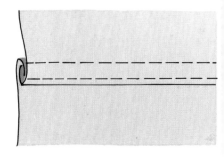

11 Trim skirt allowances to ¼in (5mm). Press seam down. Turn under bodice seam allowance to enclose waist seam and pin, baste and stitch to form waist casing.

Measurement diagram

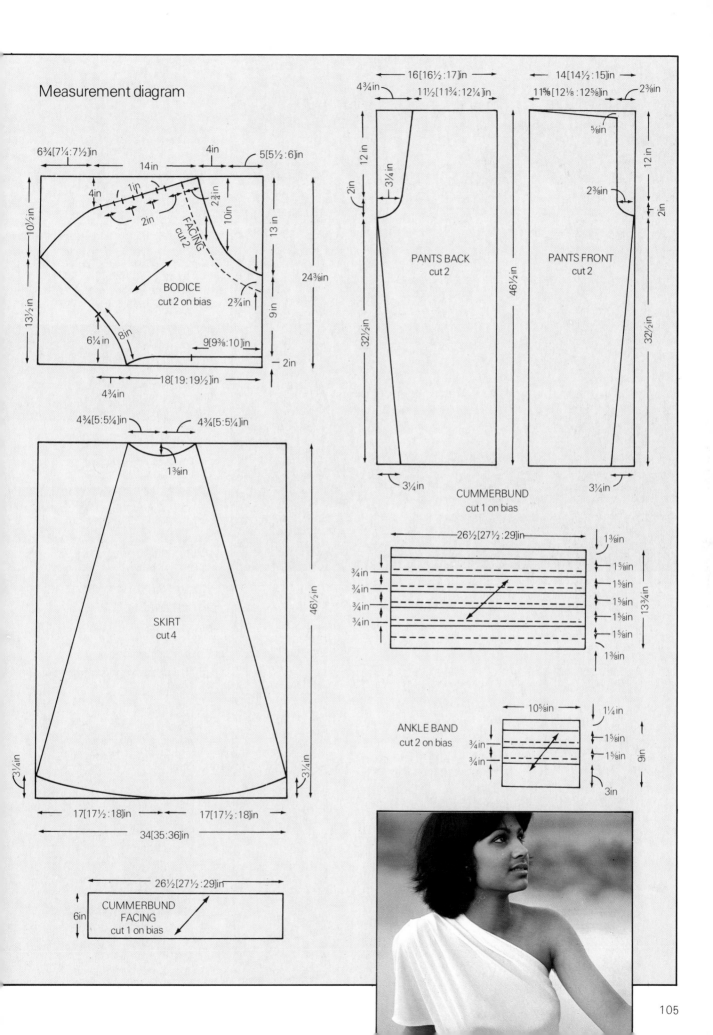

BODICE
cut 2 on bias

6¾[7¼:7½]in   14in   4in   5[5½:6]in

4in   1in   2¾in

2in

FACING
cut 2

10½in   10in   13 in   24⅜in

13½in   9in

2¾in

6¼ in   8in

9[9⅜:10]in   2in

18[19:19½]in

4¾in

SKIRT
cut 4

4¾[5:5¼]in   4¾[5:5¼]in

1⅜in

46½in

3¼in   3¼in

17[17½:18]in   17[17½:18]in

34[35:36]in

CUMMERBUND FACING
cut 1 on bias

26½[27½:29]in

6in

PANTS BACK
cut 2

16[16½:17]in

4¾in   11½[11¾:12¼]in

2in   12 in   3¼in

46½in

2in

32½in

3¼in

PANTS FRONT
cut 2

14[14½:15]in

11⅝[12⅛:12⅝]in   2⅜in

⅝in

12 in

2⅜in   2in

32½in

3¼in

CUMMERBUND
cut 1 on bias

26½[27½:29]in   1⅜in

¾in   1⅝in
¾in   1⅝in
¾in   1⅝in   13¾in
¾in   1⅝in

1⅝in

1⅜in

ANKLE BAND
cut 2 on bias

10⅝in   1¼in

¾in   1⅝in
¾in   1⅝in   9in

3in

105

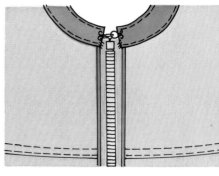

12 Insert zipper in left side. Sew facing to wrong side of zipper. Sew hook and eye at top. Thread elastic through casing and finish ends (see Technique tip). Hang skirt for a couple of days, then try for fit. Mark hem, turn up and slip stitch in place.

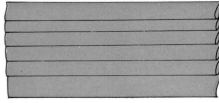

13 Working from the right side of the cummerbund make five pleats by folding along marked lines as shown and baste.

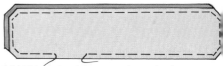

14 With right sides together, pin, baste and stitch cummerbund facing to

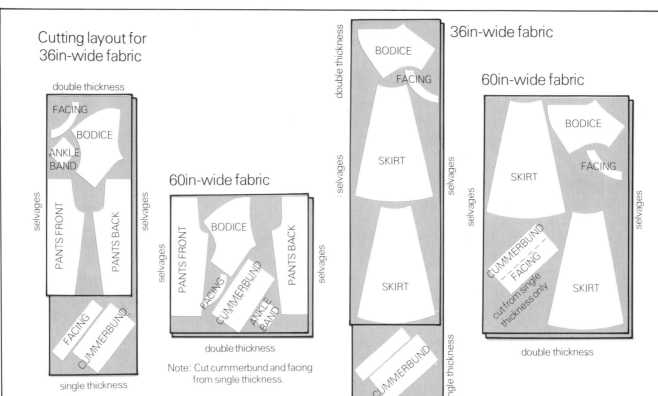

Cutting layout for 36in-wide fabric

double thickness

FACING
BODICE
ANKLE BAND
PANTS FRONT
PANTS BACK

selvages · selvages

60in-wide fabric

PANTS FRONT
BODICE
FACING
CUMMERBUND
ANKLE BAND
PANTS BACK

selvages · selvages

double thickness

Note: Cut cummerbund and facing from single thickness.

FACING
CUMMERBUND

single thickness

36in-wide fabric

double thickness

BODICE
FACING
SKIRT
SKIRT

selvages · selvages

CUMMERBUND

single thickness

60in-wide fabric

BODICE
FACING
SKIRT
SKIRT
CUMMERBUND
FACING
cut from single thickness only

selvages · selvages

double thickness

cummerbund around outer edges, leaving a gap in the stitching for turning right side out. Trim seam. Turn allowances right side out; press. Slip stitch opening.

15 Fold cummerbund in half and make a mark ¾in (2cm) toward the back from center point. At marked point run two rows of stitching close together through cummerbund and facing to secure pleats. Remove basting and press well. Sew on seven hooks and eyes or work loops at side.

Jumpsuit

Materials

5¼yd (4.8m) of 36in (90cm)-wide fabric or 3⅛yd (2.8m) of 60in (150cm)-wide fabric
14in (35cm) dress zipper
17 hooks and eyes
⅞yd (.8m) of ⅜in (1cm)-wide elastic
3in (7cm) of ⅜in (1cm)-wide tape
Matching thread, yardstick, flexible curve, paper for pattern

1 For an accurate fit it is advisable to make a paper pattern for each piece. Before cutting out, check the pants length and the crotch depth and adjust if necessary. Cut out all the pieces, following the appropriate fabric layout.
Note: Ankle bands are cut on the bias. Mark pleat lines with tailor's tacks as for cummerbund.
2 Make bodice as for the dress, following steps 2 to 8.

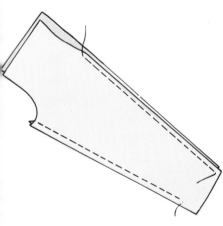

3 With right sides together, pin, baste and stitch pants fronts to backs at side seams, leaving a 7in (18cm) opening at waist edge on left side seam only. Press seams open and finish. With right sides together, pin, baste and stitch pants fronts to backs at inside leg seams, leaving a 3¼in (8cm) opening at both lower edges. Press seams open and finish.

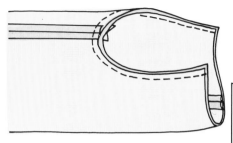

4 Turn one leg right side out and slip it inside the other leg. With right sides together and inside leg seams matching, pin, baste and stitch the crotch seam. Press seam open and finish. Run two rows of gathering around waist edge and both lower leg edges.
5 With right sides together, slip bodice inside pants and pin together at side seams and center front and back. Draw up gathers on pants to fit bodice and pin around waist seam. Baste and stitch seam, taking ¾in (2cm) seam allowances.
6 Make waist casing, insert zipper and elastic as on dress, steps 11 and 12.

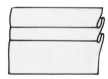

7 Working from the right side of ankle band, make two pleats by folding along lines of tailor's tacks as shown and baste.

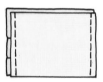 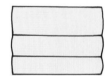

8 With right sides together, fold band in half and pin, baste and stitch at sides. Trim seams, turn right side out and press.

9 With pants wrong side out, slip ankle band inside lower edge of pants legs and draw up gathers to fit band. Distribute gathers evenly. Pin, baste and stitch pants legs to outside of band only. Trim seam. Press band upward.

10 Turn under seam allowance on free edge of band and hem in place.

Sew four hooks and eyes or work loops at side of band.
Repeat for other ankle band.
11 Make cummerbund as for dress.

Technique tip

Elasticized waist with zipper

The waist of the garments shown here are elasticized, which ensures a good fit. However, the garments also have side opening zippers, which means that the ends of the elastic have to be secured in some way. If the ends of the elastic were simply stitched to the seam allowances at the zipper opening, the elastic would tend to pull at the zipper. The answer is to secure the ends behind the zipper with a hook and eye. Since it is difficult to sew a hook and eye onto elastic, a length of tape is attached to each end of the elastic.

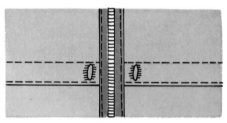

Make a slit in the inside of the casing at each end, ⅝in (1.5cm) from zipper. Finish edges with buttonhole stitch.

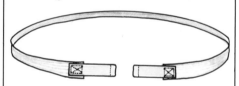

Cut a length of elastic to waist measurement, less 1⅛in (3cm). Attach a 1⅜in (3.5cm) length of tape to each end of the elastic, turning under ¼in (5mm) at each end of the tape to finish. Stitch securely to the elastic as shown.

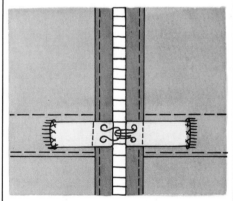

Attach a hook to one piece of tape and an eye to the other piece. Thread elastic through casing and catch-stitch in place.

Birgit Webb

107

Over-dressed

These simple-to-make pinafores come in two versions—with or without ruffles. Either version may be smocked.

Measurements

To fit ages 2/3 (chest 21/22in [53/56cm]), 4/5 (chest 23/24in [58/61cm]), and 6/7 (chest 25/26in [64/66cm]). Finished back length from neck: $21\frac{1}{2}[22\frac{1}{2}:27\frac{1}{2}$in] (55[60:70]cm).

Note: Measurements are given for ages 2/3. Figures for ages 4/5 and 6/7 are in brackets []. If only one figure is given, it applies to all sizes. $\frac{5}{8}$in (1.5cm) seam and hem allowances given; 2in (5cm) hem allowed on plain version.

Suggested fabrics

Lightweight fabrics such as lawn, batiste, challis, cotton prints, etc.

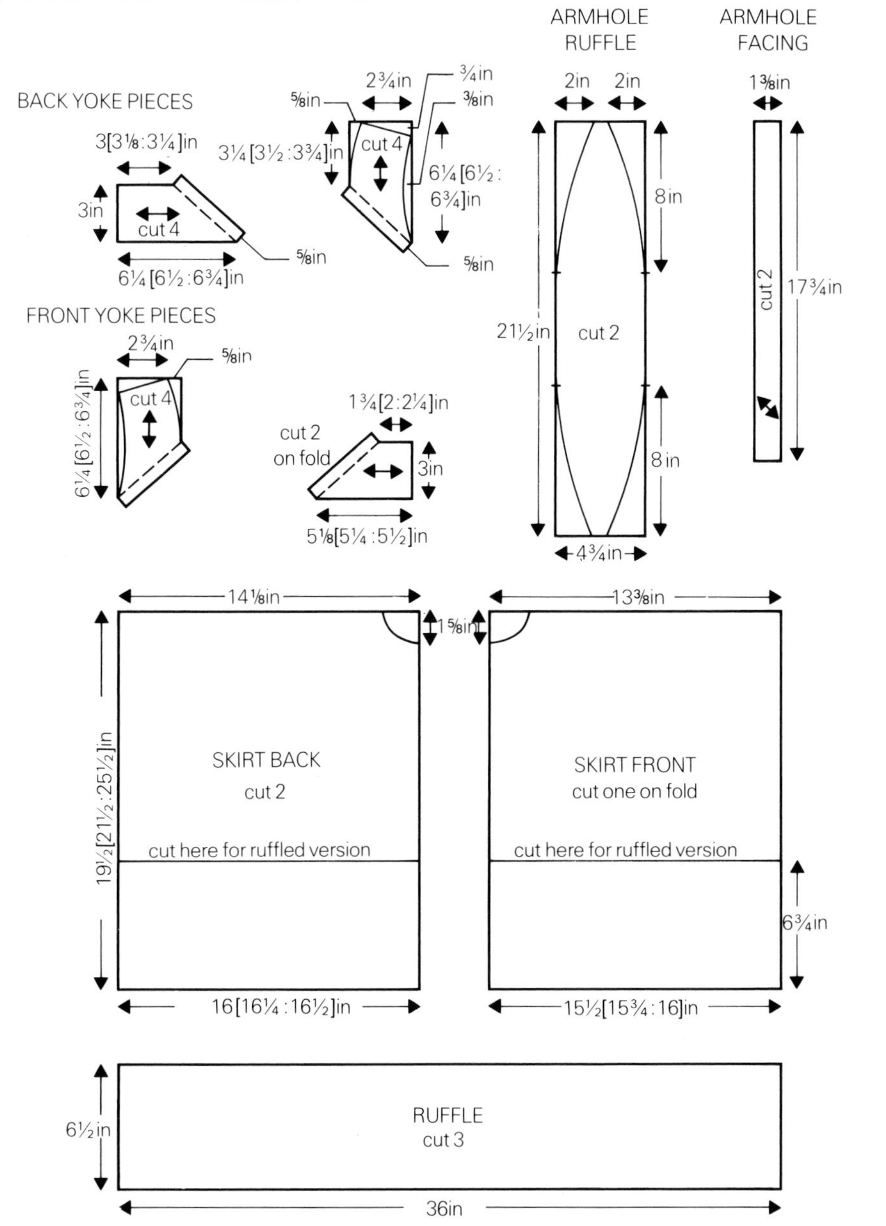
BACK YOKE PIECES
3[3⅛:3¼]in
3in
cut 4
6¼[6½:6¾]in
⅝in
2¾in
¾in
⅜in
⅝in
3¼[3½:3¾]in
cut 4
6¼[6½:6¾]in
⅝in
ARMHOLE RUFFLE
2in 2in
8in
21½in
cut 2
8in
4¾in
ARMHOLE FACING
1⅜in
cut 2
17¾in
FRONT YOKE PIECES
2¾in
⅝in
cut 4
6¼[6½:6¾]in
1¾[2:2¼]in
cut 2 on fold
3in
5⅛[5¼:5½]in
14⅛in
1⅝in
13⅜in
SKIRT BACK
cut 2
cut here for ruffled version
19½[21½:25½]in
16[16¼:16½]in
SKIRT FRONT
cut one on fold
cut here for ruffled version
6¾in
15½[15¾:16]in
RUFFLE
cut 3
6½in
36in

Cutting layout for 36in-wide fabric

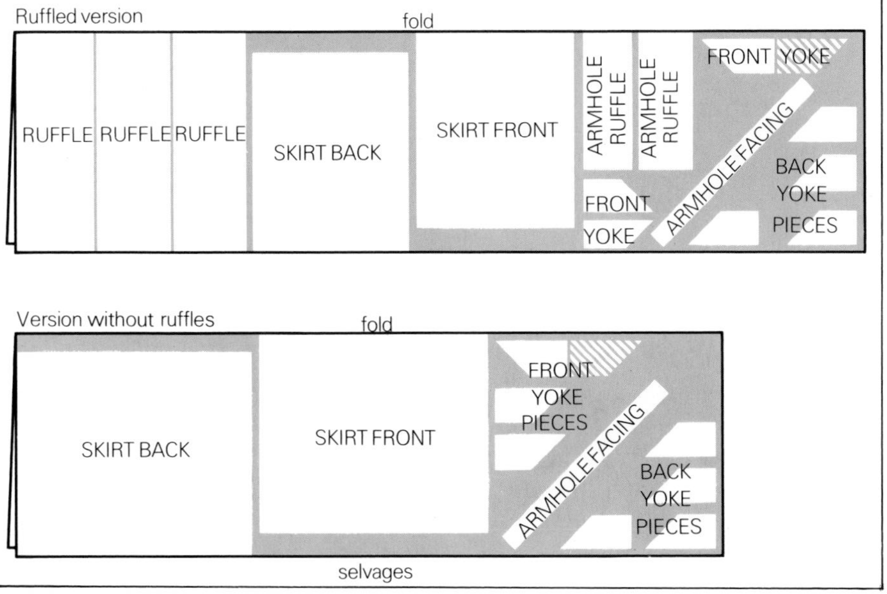
Ruffled version
fold
RUFFLE
RUFFLE
RUFFLE
SKIRT BACK
SKIRT FRONT
ARMHOLE RUFFLE
ARMHOLE RUFFLE
FRONT YOKE
ARMHOLE FACING
BACK YOKE PIECES
FRONT YOKE
Version without ruffles
fold
SKIRT BACK
SKIRT FRONT
FRONT YOKE PIECES
ARMHOLE FACING
BACK YOKE PIECES
selvages

Materials

$1\frac{5}{8}[1\frac{3}{4}:2]$yd (1.5[1.6:1.8]m) of 36in (90cm)-wide fabric for version without ruffle
$2\frac{1}{8}[2\frac{1}{4}:2\frac{3}{8}]$yd (1.9[2:2.1]m) of 36in (90cm)-wide fabric for version with ruffle
$\frac{1}{4}$yd (.2m) of 36in (90cm)-wide interfacing
Matching thread, two small buttons
Stranded embroidery floss
Transfer sheet of smocking dots $\frac{1}{4}$in (6mm) apart
Yardstick, flexible curve, tailor's chalk, paper for pattern

Note: For an accurate fit it is advisable to make a paper pattern for the yoke and armhole ruffle by following the measurement diagram. The skirt and lower ruffle can be chalked directly onto the fabric. The smocking can be used on either version.

Pinafore without ruffle

1 Following the cutting layout, cut out all the pieces. Make sure to place front skirt and yokes on a fold and to cut armhole facing on the bias.
2 To cut interfacing, join yoke pieces along marked seamline and trace a pattern for the front and a pattern for the two backs. Cut two back yoke pieces and one front yoke piece in interfacing.
3 For smocked version: from the smocking transfer, cut a rectangle $25\frac{1}{2}$in (65cm) long and 8 rows of dots deep for skirt front and two rectangles $12\frac{1}{2}$in (32cm) long and 8 rows of dots deep for skirt backs. Following directions given with transfer, iron onto wrong side of fabric $\frac{3}{4}$in (2cm) below top edge of skirt, positioned in the center of skirt front and 1in (2.5cm) in from center back raw edge on skirt backs.

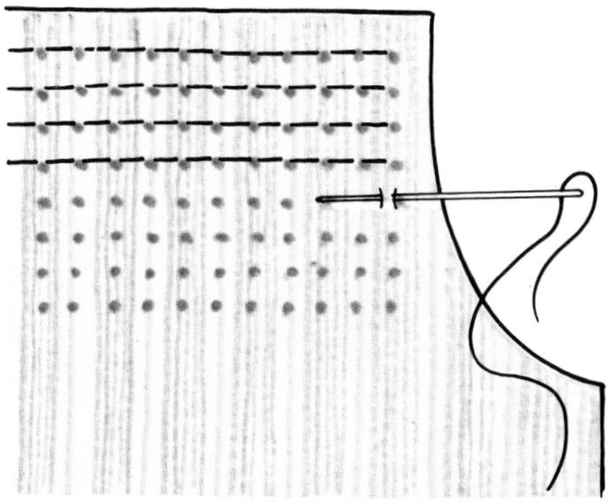

4 Gather the top of the skirt section, following the dots (see Volume 5, page 63). Draw up threads so that area to be smocked matches width of yoke.
5 Using stranded embroidery floss work five rows of smocking across the front and backs (see page 111).
6 With right sides together pin, baste and stitch skirt front to skirt backs at side seams. Press seam open and finish.

7 With right sides together and diagonal raw edges matching, join the seams to form the yoke pieces. Press seams open.

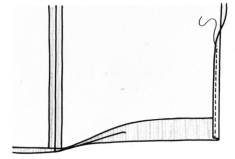

8 Turn up a 2in (5cm) hem around lower edge of skirt and slip stitch in place.
9 Turn under a ¼in (5mm) double hem down center back edges of skirt; stitch.
10 Baste interfacing to wrong side of front and back yokes.

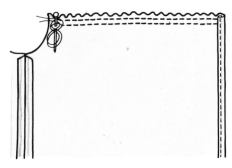

11 For unsmocked version, run two lines of gathering stitches around top of skirt and draw up gathers to fit yokes. On both versions, position center back hemmed edge of skirt 1¼in (3cm) away from center back edge of yoke to allow for extension. With right sides together, pin, baste and stitch skirt to yokes. Trim seam allowances and press toward yoke. Remove gathering threads from smocking.

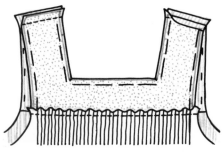

12 With right sides together pin, baste and stitch one front yoke to back yokes at shoulders. Trim interfacing close to

stitching. Trim fabric seam allowances and press seams open.
With right sides together, join remaining back yoke sections to front yoke at shoulders for yoke facing. Trim seam allowances and press open.

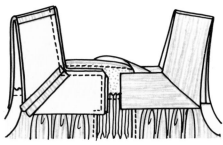

13 With right sides together, pin, baste and stitch yoke facing to yoke around neck and center back edge, continuing stitching across lower edge of back for ⅝in (1.5cm) to form extension. Trim interfacing close to stitching. Trim fabric seam allowances. Turn right side out and press.

14 Turn under seam allowances on lower edges of facing and hem in place over machine stitching. Baste facing to yoke around armhole edge.

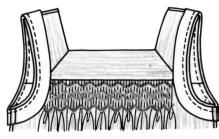

15 With right sides together, pin armhole facing around armhole edge and join neatly at underarm. Baste and stitch in place. Trim seam allowances and snip around curve.

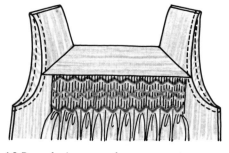

16 Press facing away from garment. Working from the right side topstitch

through facing and seam allowances only to strengthen the seam and prevent seam from rolling. Press facing to wrong side. Turn under raw edges and slip stitch to yoke facing and skirt.

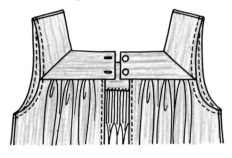

17 Make buttonholes on left back ⅝in (1.5cm) in from finished back edge and ¾in (2cm) apart. Attach buttons in corresponding positions on right back.

Pinafore with ruffles

1 Follow steps 1–7 for version without ruffles to cut out, smock the skirts and join the yoke pieces.
2 With right sides together join ruffle sections and press seams open.
3 Turn under a ⅜in (1cm) hem along one long edge and stitch.
Run two rows of gathers along other long edge of ruffle and draw up to fit lower edge of skirt, matching center of ruffle to center front of skirt; distribute the gathers evenly.
4 With right sides together, pin, baste and stitch ruffle to skirt. Trim seam allowances, overcast together and press upward; or trim ruffle seam allowances to ¼in (5mm), fold skirt allowances over to enclose seam and stitch in place.
5 Finish center back edges as in step 8 of pinafore without ruffle.
6 Follow steps 9–14 for version without ruffles to complete yoke.

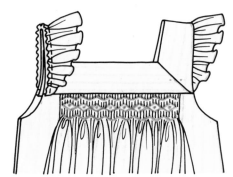

7 With right side outside, fold armhole ruffles in half lengthwise and press. Run two rows of gathers along curved edge. Draw up to fit armhole, positioning ends of ruffle at bottom of yokes and matching center of ruffle to shoulder seam. Adjust gathers and baste in place, matching raw edges of ruffle to raw edge of front and back yoke.
8 Complete as for pinafore without ruffles.

Technique tip

More smocking stitches

The pinafores shown here use a combination of stitches to give a smooth but interesting smocked band across the front.

Wave stitch

This is a simple outline stitch which is used to give a firm edge to a piece of smocking. The stitches form zig-zags, and rows may be positioned close together or a small distance apart.

Bring the needle up to the left of the first two pleats, at the left-hand side of the area to be smocked, at the level of the first gathering thread. Make a stitch to join the first two pleats and bring the needle out between the first two pleats and slightly below the first stitch.

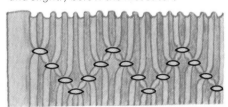

Make four or five stitches in this way, working down toward the second row of gathering. Then zig-zag back up to the first row of gathering over the same number of pleats, making the same number of stitches.

Trellis stitch

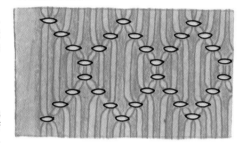

This is similar to wave stitch, but zig-zag rows are worked in opposite directions.

Bullion stitch

This is a free embroidery stitch, rather than a smocking stitch, but its bulk makes it a suitable embellishment for a smocked area. It is worked in a similar way to a French knot.

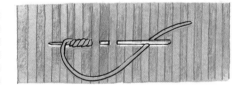

Bring the point of the needle out through one of the pleats. Wind the thread around the needle several times – the more times you wind it, the longer the bullion knot.

Draw the thread gently through the coils and take it back through the fabric on the next pleat, or through the pleat after next.

Diamond stitch

This stitch is similar to honeycomb stitch but is larger, worked over a greater number of pleats.

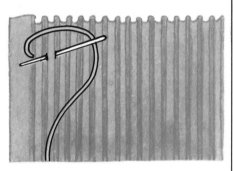

Bring the needle up to the left of the first pleat at the left-hand end of the first row of gathering. Take a backstitch through the second pleat.

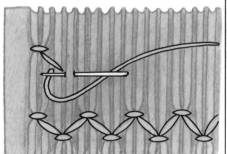

Bring the thread down to the next row of gathering on the right side of the fabric and take a backstitch through the third pleat.
Take a backstitch through the fourth pleat, and then repeat the process at the level of the first row of gathering through the fifth and sixth pleats.

Homemaker

Town and country

Stitch or knit a picture of your street or house. These examples— a town street and an English thatched cottage—show you how charming the effect can be. To complete the picture, add a matching frame.

Town street in appliqué

Finished size

8in (20.5cm) square, including frame.

Materials

Scraps of fabric in different colors and textures
Iron-on canvas or heavy interfacing
Lightweight iron-on interfacing
Thick tracing paper
Dressmaker's carbon paper
Matching sewing threads
Embroidery floss for flowers
Sharp pair of embroidery scissors

1 Trace the design from the diagram on page 114 onto the thick tracing paper; include the edge of the picture.
2 For the background/sky cut a piece of light blue fabric the size of the finished picture, plus an extra 2in (5cm) on all four edges.
3 From iron-on canvas cut a piece the same size as the background fabric. Place the shiny side of the canvas on the wrong side of the fabric. Iron in place.

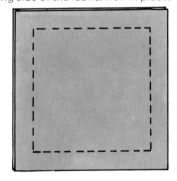

4 Mark the finished size of the picture, 6in (15.5cm) square, on the center of the background fabric with basting.
The picture is made by applying the different fabric pieces to the background fabric using a narrow machine satin stitch, following the traced lines and then trimming away the excess fabric.
To make the appliqué easier to position, always cut a piece large enough to include not only the feature being applied but also the adjacent area up to the nearest corner.

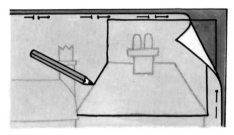

5 To mark the features on the different fabrics, first place the fabric scrap right side up, then lay a piece of dressmaker's carbon paper and the picture tracing on top, making sure that one corner of the picture can be marked on the fabric scrap. Pin all layers firmly together.
6 Trace around the chosen feature and the corner nearest to it. Remove the tracing and the carbon paper. Trim away the fabric outside the corner lines.

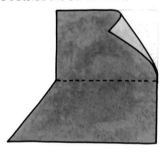

7 Before applying the pieces, stiffen each one with lightweight iron-on interfacing, to make the final trimming easier. Cut out each piece of interfacing the same size as the fabric piece. Lay the shiny side of the interfacing on the wrong side of each fabric piece. Iron in place.

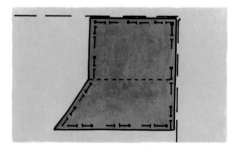

8 To fix each piece in place, align the

corner edge with the basted line at the corresponding corner on the background fabric; pin and baste in place.
9 Satin stitch by machine around the traced feature. Trim away the excess fabric using sharp scissors.

10 Apply the left-hand chimney top first, then the two outer houses and then the center house. Next add the chimneys on left-hand and center houses and the roofs on outer and center houses. Add chimney pot and chimney on last house.
11 Add the features to the three houses. Fix windows and doors, working the frames in contrasting satin stitch and making the stitching wider to give the frames more shape.
12 Next apply the street and sidewalk, marking in the curb line.

13 Add the bushes to the fronts of the houses, placing the steps to the right-hand house behind the bushes.

Terry Evans

14 Position the gate between the two bushes on the left-hand side, working a line of stitching for the top bar of the gate.

15 Next place the van in position, first placing the tires behind the bottom edge. Stitch a steering wheel in black thread and lines for the two hubcaps in pale gray thread.

16 Add a lamppost to the right-hand side, suggesting the glass with a slightly wider satin stitch, filling the area.

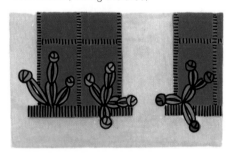

17 Embroider the flowers on the sills of the center house, using chain stitch for the stems and French knots for the flowers.

18 Give the picture a good press.

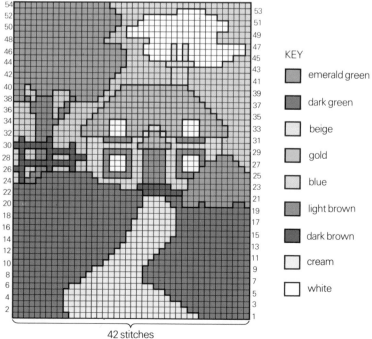

42 stitches

KEY

- emerald green
- dark green
- beige
- gold
- blue
- light brown
- dark brown
- cream
- white

114

abric frame

Materials

¼yd (.3m) of 36in (90cm)-wide
    closely-woven, medium-weight
    fabric
Piece of cardboard 8in (20.5cm)
    square
Fabric glue
Matching thread
1in (2.5cm)-diameter curtain ring
    for hanging

Trim the picture down to 8in (20.5cm)
quare to fit the cardboard. Glue the
icture to the cardboard, matching edges.
. Cut two pieces of fabric, each 8¾in
22.5cm) square.
 For frame front mark a 6in (15.5cm)
quare on one piece of fabric with basting,
entering it exactly. Cut out the center
rea, leaving a ⅜in (1cm) margin inside
he basted line, and discard.
 Place the front and back of the frame
ogether with right sides facing and edges
natching. Pin, baste and stitch around
op and sides, taking ⅜in (1cm) seam
llowance and leaving bottom edge open.
 Trim the seams and cut across the
pper corners. Turn frame right side out.
 Slip the picture into the frame. Turn in
he edges along the bottom and slip stitch
hem together neatly.
 Turn in edges around picture along
asted lines, first snipping into the
orners. Slip stitch the inner edge of the
rame to the front of the picture.
 Hand-sew the curtain ring to the back
f the frame, about 1½in (4cm) down
rom the top edge.

Country house

Size

8in (20.5cm) square, including frame.

Materials

1oz (25g) of a sport yarn in each of
    dark green, emerald green, beige,
    gold, blue, light brown, dark
    brown, cream and white
A small ball of a medium-weight
    mohair in white for cloud
Left-over lengths of red, yellow and
    orange yarn for embroidery
1 pair No. 2 (3mm) knitting needles
Large tapestry needle

Gauge

28 sts and 38 rows to 4in (10cm) in
stockinette st on No. 2 (3mm) needles.

1 Wind ball of cream into 3 small balls.
2 Using No. 2 (3mm) needles and one of
the balls of cream, cast on 56 sts for
border.
3 Work 8 rows stockinette st, so ending
with a P row.
4 Divide the ball of dark green in half
for grass sections.

5 Beg picture, twisting yarns when
changing color to prevent a hole or
stranding color not in use loosely across
WS of knitting.
6 (1st row) K7 cream for border, join on
first ball of dark green, K9 dark green,
join on 2nd ball of cream, K23 cream,
join on 2nd ball of dark green, K10 dark
green, join on 3rd ball of cream, K7
cream for border.
7 (2nd row) P7 cream, 7 dark green,
22 cream, 11 dark green, 7 cream.
8 Cont in stockinette st with border in
cream at each end, working from row 3
of chart until the 54th row has been
worked.
9 Cont with cream only, work 8 rows
stockinette st. Bind off. Press on WS.
10 Using tapestry needle and gold yarn
work stem stitch over roof section and
above door, working into each side of
stitches, for thatched look, then overcast
all around edge of roof.
11 With beige yarn embroider French
knot on door for handle.
12 With red yarn embroider French knots
on tree for apples.
13 With yellow and orange yarn embroider
French knots on grass for flowers.
14 With light brown yarn work long
stitches across windows for frames.

Knitted frame

Materials

2oz (50g) of a sport yarn in brick
1 pair of No. 2 (3mm) knitting
    needles
Piece of thick batting 9in (23cm)
    square

8in (20.5cm) square of cardboard
Fabric glue
One 1in (2.5cm)-diameter curtain
    ring, for hanging

Gauge

28 sts and 38 rows to 4in (10cm) in
stockinette st on No. 2 (3mm) needles.

1 Using No. 2 (3mm) needles cast on 58 sts.
2 Work 10 rows stockinette st, so ending
with a P row.
3 Next row K8, bind off 42, K8.
4 Cont in stockinette st on last set of 8
sts for 6in (15.5cm); end with a P row.
5 Cut off yarn and leave rem sts on a
spare needle.
6 Return to first set of 8 sts. With WS
facing rejoin yarn to first st and P to
end of row.
7 Cont in stockinette st for 6in (15.5cm);
end with a P row.
8 Next row K to end, turn and cast on
42 sts, turn again and onto same needle
K the sts from spare needle. 58 sts.
9 Work 9 rows. Mark each end of last
row to denote completion of front. Cont
in stockinette st for back, until back is
same length as front. Bind off. Press
lightly on WS if required.
10 Using the front section of frame as a
template, cut batting.
11 With RS tog, join side seams of
frame, turn RS out.
12 Mount picture on cardboard.
13 Insert picture into frame, then insert
batting and slip stitch opening.
14 Slip stitch around inner edge of frame.
15 Hand sew curtain ring to center back
of frame, about 1½in (4cm) down from top.

Homemaker

Studio style

Ideal for a studio apartment or a guest room, this fitted bedspread has corded edges and a box pleated skirt.

Finished size
To fit a bed 6ft 3in × 36in (1.9m × 90cm). Height to top of mattress, 21in (53cm). A seam allowance of $\frac{3}{4}$in (2cm) has been included throughout.

Materials
9$\frac{1}{8}$yd (8.4m) of 48in (122cm)-wide printed furnishing fabric
13yd (12m) of filler cord
Matching thread

1 For top cut a piece of fabric 76$\frac{1}{2}$ × 37$\frac{1}{2}$in (194×95cm). For sides cut two pieces, each 76$\frac{1}{2}$ × 9$\frac{1}{2}$in (194×24cm), and two pieces, each 37 × 9$\frac{1}{2}$in (95×24cm). For skirt cut nine pieces, each 48 × 15$\frac{1}{2}$in (122×40cm).

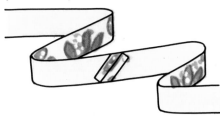

2 From the remaining fabric cut out 2in (5cm)-wide strips on the bias for cording. Pin, baste and stitch the strips with right sides together to make a strip about 12$\frac{1}{2}$yd (11.5m) long.
3 Fold the strip in half around the filler cord, right side out and with edges matching. Pin, baste and stitch close to the cord to hold it firmly in place. Cut the length of cording in half.

4 Pin the cording around all four edges at base of the top piece, beginning at one corner and placing the cording with its edges aligned with edges of top piece.

5 Curve the cording slightly around each corner, snipping into the cording seam allowance to help it curve easily. Cut off excess cording; pin, baste and sew the ends together to fit. Baste and stitch cording in place.

6 Place one long side piece and one short side piece together at one end, with right sides facing. Pin, baste and stitch the two together.
7 Repeat step 6 with remaining two side pieces.

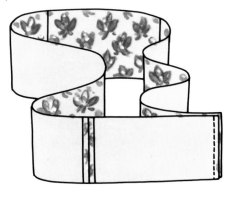

8 Place the two combined side pieces together with right sides facing and short and long sides alternating. Pin, baste and stitch the two remaining seams. Press seams flat and finish them.

Terry Evans

9 Place side piece on top piece over corded edge, with right sides together, edges matching and seams meeting corners exactly. Pin, baste and stitch in place, using a cording foot if possible.

10 Pin the remaining length of cording around the remaining raw edge of side piece, starting at one corner and placing the cording with its edges aligned with the edges of the side piece. Pin, baste and sew the cording ends together to fit. Baste and stitch the cording in place.

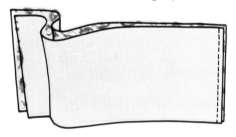

11 Place two skirt pieces together with right sides facing and edges matching. Pin, baste and stitch along one edge.

12 Repeat step 11 to join all skirt pieces into one long strip. Press seams open.

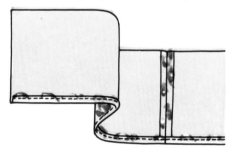

13 Turn under ⅜in (1cm) on one long edge of skirt. Pin and stitch in place.

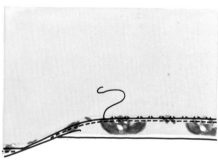

14 Turn up this finished edge another 1¼in (3cm). Pin, baste and hem in place by hand.

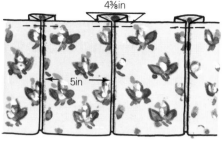

15 Pin and baste box pleats on the skirt. Beginning at one end, mark off ¾in (2cm) seam allowance, then 2¼in (5.5cm) for half of the under section of the first pleat. Then mark off 5in (12.5cm) for top of first pleat, then 4⅜in (11cm) for the next (complete) under section. Continue marking until you have 15 pleats, adjusting the marks if necessary so that each fabric width contains five pleats exactly. Pin and baste pleats in place. Mark, pin and baste the next seven pleats in the same way, but make the six under sections about 4in (10.2cm) wide, so that these pleats will fit the short end of the cover.

Mark, pin and baste another group of

15 pleats and another group of seven, as before. Trim away the fabric at the end of the skirt, leaving enough to complete the under section of the first pleat. Seam the two free edges and press seam open.

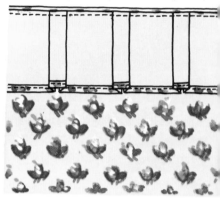

16 Place the skirt on the corded edge of side piece with sides, top and base edges matching and right sides together. Ease the pleats to fit the cover where necessary. Pin, baste and stitch the skirt in place. Press seam upward.

Homemaker

Suffolk puff crib quilt

This unusual kind of patch-work, of English origin, is called Suffolk puffs. For warmth, the puffs in this quilt are stuffed with batting. The quilt is machine-washable.

Finished size
23 × 17½in (58 × 44cm).
Each finished puff measures about 2in (5cm) in diameter.

Materials
¾yd (.7m) of 36in (90cm)-wide patterned lightweight nylon fabric
1yd (1m) of 36in (90cm)-wide white lightweight nylon fabric
⅞yd (.8m) of 36in (90cm)-wide pale blue lightweight nylon fabric
¾yd (.7m) of 36in (90cm)-wide polyester batting
Matching synthetic thread
Six 1in (2.5cm)-diameter lace motifs
Stiff paper
Pencil
Compass

1 On the wrong side of each piece of nylon, using a soft pencil and a compass, draw 3½in (9cm)-diameter circles for the puffs, leaving at least ½in (1.2cm) between each circle. Draw 52 on the patterned blue fabric, 78 on the white fabric and 58 on the pale blue fabric.
2 Cut out each fabric circle, adding ¼in (6mm) allowance all around for seams.
3 Also from the nylon fabric cut out 1½in (4cm)-diameter circles for the batting covers, cutting 52 in patterned blue, 78 in white and 58 in pale blue.
4 From batting cut out 188 pieces, each 2in (5cm) square, for filling.

in the corners of the batting to fit the fabric cover. Pin and baste firmly in place.
6 Repeat step 5 to baste each batting square to each batting cover to form the padded centers.

7 On one puff fabric piece, turn in the allowance all around the circle. Pin and baste. Thread a fine needle with a length of thread. Knot unthreaded end and, starting with a backstitch, run a line of gathering stitches around the folded edge of the circle.

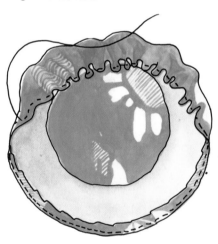

8 Center a covered piece of batting, fabric side up, on wrong side of gathered circle. Draw up gathering thread around batting piece as tightly as possible. Take a few invisible stitches through puff to anchor batting in place and fasten off gathering thread securely.
9 Repeat steps 7 and 8 to make the rest of the puffs.
10 To help in assembling the quilt, cut out paper hexagons with 1in (2.5cm)-long side edges. You will need 188, but each paper template can be used many times, so draw about 20 to start with, following steps 11-15, and make more later if necessary.
11 On stiff paper, using a pencil and compass, draw a circle with a 1in (2.5cm) radius.

Ron Kelly

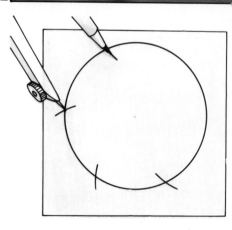

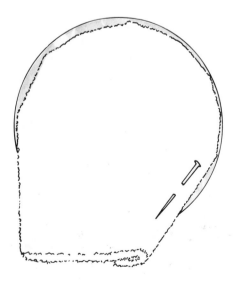

5 Place one batting square on wrong side of one batting cover piece, turning

12 With the compass still open at the same radius, place the compass point on the edge of the circle. Mark another point farther along the circumference, 1in (2.5cm) from where the compass point is positioned.

18 Place two puffs together with gathered sides (right sides) facing. Overcast the puffs together along one side of the hexagon, to within $\frac{1}{8}$in (3mm) of the corners. Remove the paper hexagons.

19 Repeat step 18 to sew puffs together to form the quilt. Start at the center with a broad row of pale blue. On each side of the center, sew one row of white, one of patterned blue, one of white, a broad row of pale blue, one of white and one of patterned blue.

13 Move the compass point to this marked point and make another mark on the circle. Continue until the circle has been marked with six points.
14 Join up these points to form a hexagon.

many more hexagons as you feel you will need.

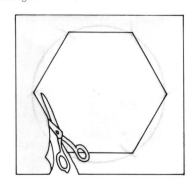

15 Carefully cut out the hexagon.
16 Repeat steps 11 to 15 to make as

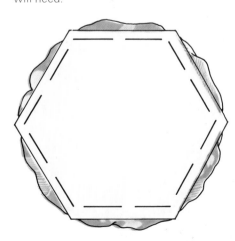

17 Baste a paper hexagon to the ungathered side of each fabric puff.

20 Sew lace motifs to pale blue center row of puffs.

Terri Lawlor

121

Homemaker

Carry baby in perfect comfort in this sling, and leave your hands free for carrying the shopping or holding a small child's hand.

Baby sling

A seam allowance of ⅜in (1cm) has been included throughout.

Materials
1yd (.9m) of 48in (122cm)-wide firmly-woven fabric
Two 2¾in (7cm)-diameter wooden rings
Scrap of medium-weight batting
Matching thread; tracing paper

1 Trace patterns for main piece and headrest from patterns on pages 124-125. Add 2¼in (6cm) to the main piece where shown to make the complete pattern: continue both long edges from broken line and join the points with a straight line.
2 From fabric cut out two main pieces and two headrest pieces. Cut out three straps, each 48×4in (122×10cm) and two 12×4in (30×10cm).

3 Place the two main pieces together with right sides facing. Pin, baste and stitch side seams.

4 Turn the main piece right side out. Pin and baste, close to the stitched edges. Using a larger-than-average stitch, topstitch along both sides, close to the edges. Topstitch down both sides again, about ⅜in (1cm) from the edges.

5 Place the headrest pieces together with right sides facing and edges matching. Pin, baste and stitch along the curved edge. Clip into the seam allowance.

6 Open the headrest out flat. Position one short edge of one 48in (122cm)-long strap at one end of the headrest piece, with right sides together. Pin, baste and stitch.
7 Repeat step 6 on the opposite side of the headrest piece with another 48in (122cm)-long strap.

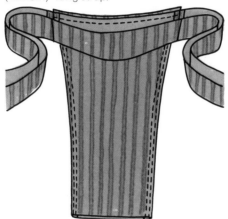

8 Place one long straight edge of headrest piece on the curved edge of main piece, with right sides together. Pin, baste and stitch together through both thicknesses of main piece.

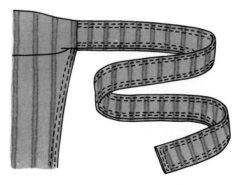

9 Turn ⅜in (1cm) to wrong side around remaining edges of one of the long straps; press. Fold strap in half, wrong sides inside. Pin and baste around the edges. Topstitch around strap, close to the edge. Topstitch around the strap again, about ⅜in (1cm) in from the edge.
10 Repeat step 9 with other long strap.

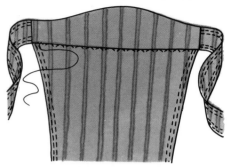

11 Trim ⅝in (1.5cm) from all edges of the headrest pattern. Using this trimmed pattern, cut out two pieces from batting. Place the two batting headrest pieces together, edges matching. Baste together around the edge. Place the batting inside the headrest and pin it in place.

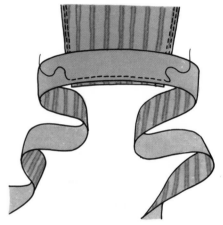

12 Turn in ⅜in (1cm) along the remaining straight edge of the headrest. Pin, baste and sew in place along existing stitching line.

13 Center the remaining long strap along the base edges of the main piece, with one long edge of strap along base edge and right sides together. Pin, baste and stitch in place.
14 Turn ⅜in (1cm) to wrong side on remaining edges of strap; press. Fold strap in half, wrong sides inside. Pin, baste and topstitch all around strap, close to the edge. Topstitch again, about ⅜in (1cm) from the edge.

15 Make the short straps: fold one short strap in half lengthwise, with right sides together. Pin, baste and stitch one short and long edge. Clip across the corner. Turn strap right side out. Pin, baste and topstitch the three closed sides close to the edge. Topstitch around the strap again, about ⅜in (1cm) from edge.
16 Repeat step 15 on other short strap.

Terry Evans

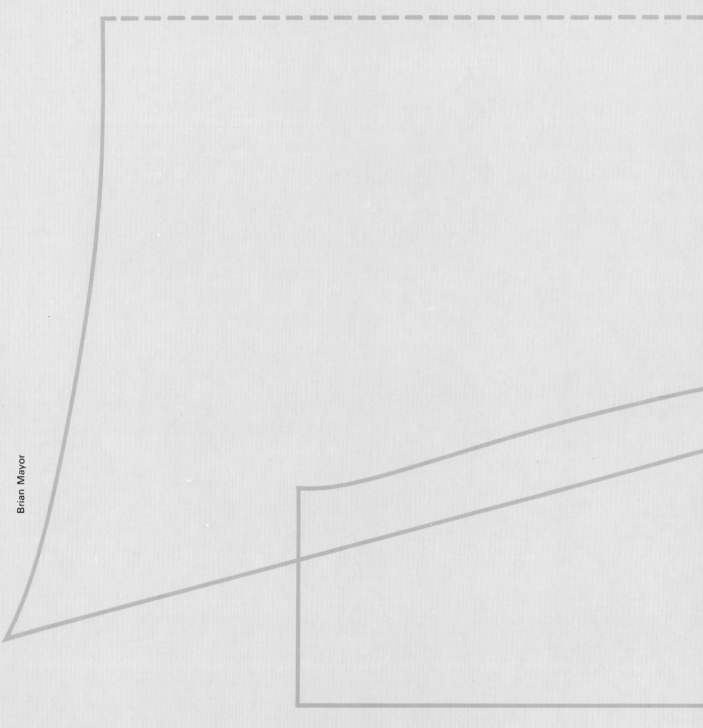

Brian Mayor

Terry Evans

17 Mark a point 1¼in (3cm) from center of long base strap. Place closed end of one short strap at this mark. Pin, baste and stitch end of strap in place, following existing lines of topstitching and re-inforcing the stitching by working from corner to corner in an "X" shape.

18 Repeat step 17 with stitched end of other short strap.

19 Thread one open end of one short strap through one wooden ring and fold it back on the strap. Pin, baste and stitch it firmly to strap using a closed zig-zag stitch.

20 Repeat step 19 to attach other wooden ring to end of remaining short strap in the same way.
21 To wear the sling: place the sling flat on a surface with the short straps against the flat surface. Place the baby on the sling. Bring the lower edge of the sling through the baby's legs. Turn the baby and sling over and tie the baby firmly in the sling. Position the baby against the front of the body. Put the long left-hand strap over the left shoulder, across the back and through the right-hand ring. Put the long right-hand strap over the right shoulder, across the back and through the left-hand ring. Pull the straps together; tie a firm knot at the back.

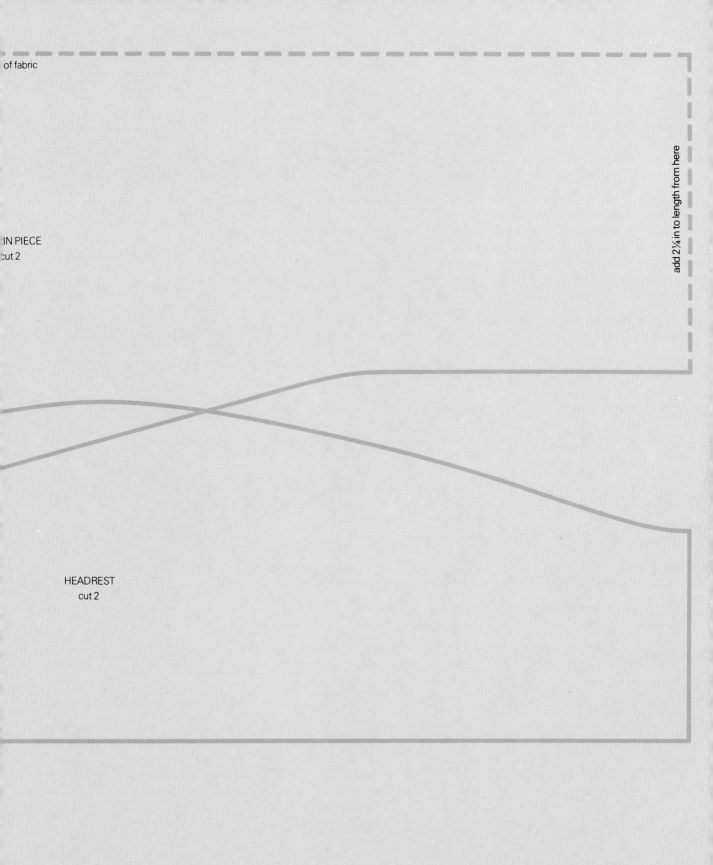

of fabric

add 2¼ in to length from here

IN PIECE
cut 2

HEADREST
cut 2

Add the finishing touch to our windows with a valance to match your draperies. Valances may be pleated or—for an informal effect—gathered. Another kind of valance consists of a flat, stiffened piece of fabric, sometimes decoratively shaped, which is hung from a narrow shelf.

Pleated or gathered valance

Materials

Main fabric—enough for the chosen heading tape (taking into account any pattern repeats)
Similar amount of lining fabric
Heading tape with drapery hooks (choose the same heading for both draperies and valance)
Double drapery rod
Matching thread

Estimate the fabric width in the same way as for the draperies (see page 59). Decide on the valance depth and add ⅜in (1cm) at each side and 2½in (6.5cm) to the depth measurements for top and bottom hems.

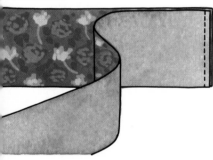

Cut out and join fabric pieces to make a strip of the required measurements. Join the widths with flat seams in the same way as for draperies, matching any pattern repeats (see Volume 1, page 117).
Cut out and seam the lining in the same way as the main fabric, but make it 3½in (9cm) shorter.

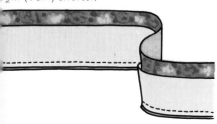

Place the main fabric and lining together with right sides facing and one long edge matching. Pin, baste and stitch the long edge taking ⅜in (1cm) seam allowance. Press seam open.

6 Move the seam up so that it is ¾in (2cm) from lower edge. Press and pin in place.

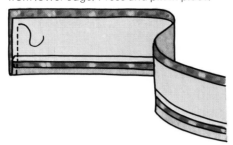

7 Match side edges together. Pin, baste and stitch side seams. Trim seams and turn the valance right side out.
8 Turn under 1⅜in (3.5cm) along the top edge of the fabric. Pin and baste along the folded edge.

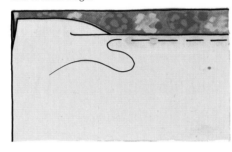

9 Turn under ⅜in (1cm) on the free edge of the lining and pin it to the fabric. The folded edge of the lining will be 1in (2.5cm) below the upper edge. Baste.

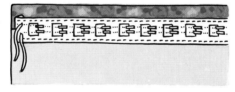

10 Place the heading tape on the wrong side of the valance with the top edge ¾in (2cm) down from the top, so that it covers the folded edge of the lining. Turn in ends of tape for ⅜in (1cm); pin, baste and stitch in place. The tape shown is for a gathered heading. If using pleater tape, take care to position it so that pleats fall at the desired places.
11 Pull up tape cords to correct width and insert hooks. Or insert pleater hooks. Hang the valance over draperies.

Shaped valance

Materials

Plywood for valance shelf
Angle iron brackets
Main fabric and lining as required
Heavyweight iron-on interfacing or buckram
Tassel trimming (optional) and braid
Matching thread
Touch-and-close fastening
Fabric glue
Graph paper; felt-tip pen

1 Cut a valance shelf from plywood, making it at least 4in (10cm) wide, to leave enough clearance for the drapery hardware.
2 To calculate the length of the valance shelf, measure the length of the drapery rod and add an extra 2in (5cm) to each side.

3 Fix the shelf to the wall just above the window with angle irons spaced at about 3in (8cm) intervals along the complete length, fixing the first two at each end of the shelf.
4 To calculate the length of the finished valance, measure the length of the shelf including the shelf returns (distance to wall) at the side edges.
5 Cut a piece of graph paper slightly larger than the valance measurements.

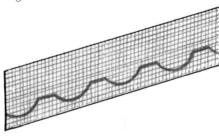

6 Draw the shape of the valance full size in pencil on the graph paper. Remember to allow the correct space for the return on each side. Use a plate or compass for help in drawing any curves. Adjust the design if necessary, then go over the lines with felt-tip pen. Cut a strip of interfacing the correct length (butting strips together if necessary) and lay it shiny side up over the graph paper. Tape it in place, then trace the pattern onto it. Cut out the interfacing shape.

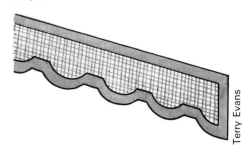

7 From the main fabric, using the interfacing as a pattern, cut out one piece, ⅝in (1.5cm) larger all around than the

Terry Evans

interfacing, first joining fabric widths together with flat seams, if necessary, to gain the required width, matching any pattern repeats.

8 Using the interfacing as a pattern, cut out one piece of lining fabric $\frac{3}{8}$in (1cm) larger than the interfacing all around, first joining the widths together as for the main fabric, if necessary.

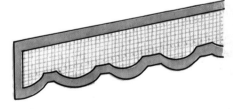

9 Place the interfacing on top of the wrong side of the main valance piece, shiny side down, centering it accurately. Press it in place.

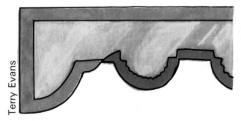

Terry Evans

10 Snip into the seam allowance all around the curved edges (if any) on the main valance piece. Fold the seam allowance over the edge of the interfacing, mitering the corners, and press it in place.

11 Turn under $\frac{5}{8}$in (1.5cm) seam allowance all around the lining. Clip into the seam allowance on curved edges.

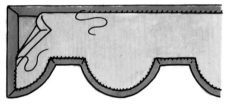

12 Place the lining on the wrong side of the valance, leaving a $\frac{1}{4}$in (5mm) margin around all edges. Baste it in place. Slip stitch the lining to the main fabric around the folded edges.
13 Position tassel trimming, if desired, along the lower edge on the right side of the valance; pin in place, then glue it down carefully.

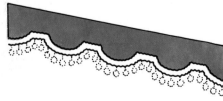

14 Position the braid along the lower edge on the right side of the valance, just over the edge of the tassel trimming, neatly folding the braid at the corners; pin and glue it in place.

15 Cut a length of touch-and-close fastening the same length as the top straight edge of the valance. Separate the fastening strips.

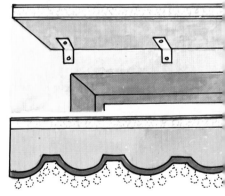

16 Glue one of the fastening strips to the shelf, beginning at the wall, so as to include the returns at each side.
17 Place the other half of the fastening on the wrong side of the valance along the top edges, matching long edges neatly together. Pin, baste and sew it in place by hand.
18 Fix the valance to the shelf by pressing the fastening strips together.

Note Buckram can be used for the valance instead of iron-on interfacing. In this case, cut the buckram to the correct size and shape as described in step 6, cut the main fabric and lining pieces as in steps 7 and 8, then catch-stitch the buckram to the wrong side of the main piece.